Secret Destinations

A JOURNEY ONLY YOU CAN TAKE

Non-fiction

Diana M. Mohrsen

One Printers Way
Altona, MB R0G 0B0
Canada

www.friesenpress.com

Copyright © 2022 by Diana M. Mohrsen
First Edition — 2022

All rights reserved.

No part of this publication may be reproduced in any form, or by any means, electronic or mechanical, including photocopying, recording, or any information browsing, storage, or retrieval system, without permission in writing from FriesenPress.

ISBN
978-1-03-913690-8 (Hardcover)
978-1-03-913689-2 (Paperback)
978-1-03-913691-5 (eBook)

1. TRAVEL, ESSAYS & TRAVELOGUES

Distributed to the trade by The Ingram Book Company

To my grandchildren: Ashlynn, Hannah, Jessica, and Zach

Adventures shared and cherished

Acknowledgments

I'd like to thank Alex McGilvery (Celticfrog Editing) for his input, Heidi Champagne (Champagne Productions) for the map designs, and Kate de Oude at FriesenPress for guiding me through the publishing process. Much gratitude to Heather England and Barb Pyner for their encouragement and feedback on earlier drafts. Also, to my friends who have suggested my solo road trips are a sign of bravery, I appreciate the opportunity to explain it is curiosity and a love of beauty, not bravery, fueling my adventures.

All journeys have secret destinations of which the traveler is unaware.

MARTIN BUBER

BEFORE THE TRIP

The Call to Adventure

THERE IS A FINE ART to adventure. It lives on the edge of the unknown. Once I realized that, I have been finding ways to experience the heady rush of adrenalin while remaining as safe as reasonably possible. Travelling to the Himalayas or other foreign lands is not necessary if I want to encounter adventure. It is everywhere—if I know where to look.

Adventure can also be found in the commonplace. There is far too much detail in our surroundings for our senses to take in everything. We automatically filter out much of the known, the ordinary. But if we practice now and then paying extraordinary attention to anything we're familiar with, we soon find ourselves in the midst of mystery. I speak from personal experience. I used to take our whole landscape for granted—as mere background for my life. Discovering what is hidden in plain sight has added a dimension of meaning for me. I have felt encouraged to explore new paths and to seek out the beauty waiting to be discovered.

The adventurous spirit has no expiry date. We can tap into it at any age. What follows is my journal of eight days exploring highways in British Columbia and Alberta. I'm writing this chapter before the trip, yet I'm certain I will experience the feeling of adventure. I don't yet know what those adventures will be. I'll describe my journey as it unfolds, and I'll share some photos from along the way. I'll be travelling alone, something not everyone is comfortable doing. When I'm on my own, I find there's an almost meditative quality to my road trips, quite different than when travelling with a companion.

I suspect some people are unaware of the joys available by merely stepping outside their comfort zones now and then. It is for these readers I am writing this book. That used to be me. But over the years, I've learned to trust that I can be both cautious and daring.

I'm not suggesting anyone follow the same route I take; I cannot promise others will see the sights that delight me, and surely our tastes will differ. Every trip is unique to the person travelling. But nevertheless, I encourage you to set out on your own adventure and to see your surroundings with fresh eyes. You may discover a sense of wonderment in unexpected places.

Anticipation

There's an aspect to adventure every bit as important as where we choose to go: the anticipation of the trip. The days of planning and researching, of figuring out just exactly what the dream is, those days are already tinged with adventure. It is on the horizon. We are stepping out to meet it.

Over twelve years ago, I purchased a commercial property in Chetwynd, and each year I've done an annual inspection and met with the tenants. Sometimes I've flown to nearby Fort St. John and rented a car. At other times, I've taken road trips, exploring B.C. and Alberta along the way. In 2020, I wasn't able to go because of Covid 19. I've been anticipating the spring of 2021 for a long time now, never suspecting that circumstances would not have changed.

Usually, I travel solo, but several years ago I discovered my oldest granddaughter is a kindred spirit and wonderful travel companion. Every time I see a bear, a herd of elk, or amazing scenery, I remember her elation at spotting wildlife along the roadside and wonder how I can share the experience with others. During the long winter of 2020, isolated in my tiny bubble, I needed something to aim towards. I decided to chronicle my journey in the spring of 2021 and create a book. Talk about stepping out into the unknown. That goal has been part of my life for some time now. I may be travelling alone on this trip but it is with the intention of inviting along anyone who might be interested.

Difficulties

There will be things to overcome in any journey, and it's never certain just what will arise. Yesterday, in response to a recall notice from Acura, I went to the dealership to have my car checked out for a possible driveshaft failure. I had assumed there would be no problem, but the technician said it needs to be replaced. All under warranty, of course, but it is a little sobering. The work is scheduled for next Wednesday, just days before I start out. What if the recall letter had reached me a couple of weeks later, after I had embarked on a four thousand kilometre journey? Could my driveshaft have cracked while I was driving? Well, that isn't what happened, so I have to be grateful for the chronological order of things. Life is a risky business, and it is fortunate we don't always know how risky or we'd have no peace.

The world is still in the midst of a pandemic caused by Covid 19. Here in B.C., we have been under various prohibitions and travel restrictions. Currently, travel outside one's health region is prohibited except for work. I feel trapped by the current circumstances. My tolerance for everything that has happened seems very precarious. There is a certain freedom, a oneness with the world, I experience on the open road. I rationalize that part of my income is based on maintaining my building in Chetwynd and ensuring my tenants are satisfied, so technically I will be travelling for work. But if I get caught in an RCMP roadblock, will they accept my explanation? Also, there is just a small window of opportunity when the bears come out of hibernation and are often spotted by the roadside. The time is now. I don't want to wait for another year. I have had my first Covid vaccination but not my second. Somehow, I have to negotiate the outside world of gas stations, hotels, and eating establishments while remaining safe. I feel confident I can do it, but it is an added concern.

Planning

My car has been serviced. I've had an oil change, brake check, wheel alignment, and air filters changed according to the maintenance schedule. In the trunk of the car, I carry hiking boots, a road hazard sign, collapsible shovel, window cleaner, paper towels, and first aid supplies. I have a good road map as well as GPS.

I found a tape recorder in my junk drawer. It's been there forever, and I can no longer remember why I purchased it. I replaced the batteries and tested it out. It seems to work just fine. My plan is to use it to record some of my observations as I travel.

My camera is fully charged. I have a little Nikon Coolpix P100 with a wide 26x zoom. I paid less than three hundred dollars for it new at least eight years ago, maybe much longer. I'm happy to use this camera instead of investing in a more expensive one because the pictures I take will be of a quality that anyone could have taken.

There is a line between chaos and order. Even though I've not yet left home, I'm already skirting that line of uncertainty. The car dealership calls to cancel my Wednesday appointment. It seems one of the necessary parts for the replacement of the driveshaft is out of stock. Momentary panic. But my trip! I can't go with a faulty driveshaft. The mechanic assures me that a long trip is not out of the question. There is no imminent danger of it failing. He sounds sincere. I'll soon be stepping out into the unknown. This just brings a finer edge to things. I do not know what I will find out there on the highway. Perhaps it will all be disappointing—no animal sightings, bad weather, heavy traffic, car problems. These things exist as possibilities. But other possibilities exist as well. A grizzly at the roadside, shafts of sunlight, scenery that enchants. These are all unknowns. I'm hopeful, yet cautious. I'm optimistic, yet practical. I've weighed my options and now I'll take my chances. It is possible things won't work out, but I've noticed in the past that things generally do. I'm thinking of this heightened tension or uncertainty as part of the flavour of adventure. I can carry on under the cloud of uncertainty. Then, if it all comes together, such elation.

DAY ONE – Saturday, June 5, 2021

From Surrey to Hope, B.C.

IT'S 10:50 ON A BRIGHT, sunny morning as I back out of my driveway in Surrey, B.C. Surrey is part of the Metro Vancouver area in the most western province of Canada. It's a city with a population of over 580,000, and in land size, it is the largest city in Canada. It lies tucked in between the border of Washington State to the south and the Fraser River to the north.

A few years ago, I spent ten days in Iceland. It always amuses me to consider that the entire population of Iceland—the city of Reykjavik and all the scattered communities around the island—is only around 365,000. I sometimes think of that as I go about my day-to-day living. There are more than enough people in Surrey to run an entire country, at least one the size of Iceland. Enough people to have an international voice with a membership in the United Nations. And yet here in Canada, we are merely a bedroom community for the city of Vancouver.

As I leave home, my odometer reads 159,001. I head east on Highway 1, part of the Trans-Canada Highway. Between Surrey and Abbotsford, a distance of forty-six kilometres, I scarcely notice much as this is such a familiar route for me. One of the main reasons I love to travel is to shake off the familiarity that blinds us to much of our surroundings. It's not that I'm ungrateful for the beauty of the North Shore Mountains or the pastoral Fraser Valley farmland, it's just that most minds, like mine, automatically dismiss the familiar and wonder instead why traffic is slowing. *Is there a problem up ahead?*

The landscape opens up around Abbotsford. From a vantage point on the highway, there is the dramatic glacier-covered Mount Baker to my right. This mountain, part of the Cascade Range, is located just across the border in the United States and is visible from many places in the lower mainland. It almost feels like it's really our mountain because it's such a feature of our landscape. For a few minutes, I'm looking down over farmland, beautiful in all the shades of green created by pastures, freshly planted fields, and trees. Beyond that is the blue of the hills and lesser mountains fading into the grey-blue of the mountains beyond that. There is the azure sky sprinkled with quite a few white clouds. Almost an hour away from home, I'm now alive to the scenery. Beyond this point feels like an adventure.

I first fell in love with paved roads as a child living in Prince Edward Island. Our farm ran the length of a dusty side road and that is where I walked to school. That is where I biked. Our school was on our small road but further along near the highway. The red clay road would get graded a couple of times a year and in between, it would settle into ruts of dried mud after a rain, or in dryer weather, parts of the road dissolved into sand. The bicycle wheels would lose traction in the sand, and I'd sink into a slow-motion struggle to maintain momentum. Biking was better than walking to school, but it still felt physically challenging.

Just before we moved to Nova Scotia when I was around eleven years old, my parents asked me to take something to family friends who lived just across the highway at the end of our road. Because this had never happened before, my mother and father gave me careful instructions about what to do when I came to the highway, how I was to bike along the pavement until I was opposite their driveway, check both ways, then quickly cross.

When my bicycle tires hit the smooth surface of a paved road after years on a lumpy, bumpy, sandy country road, well, it was a revelation. I can still remember the sound of my tires singing on the pavement. Biking seemed effortless. The whole thing was dream like. With roads like this, I thought, I could go anywhere in the world.

I exit the freeway at a rest stop just east of Abbotsford to do my first tape recording. I plan to record some impressions of the trip as they occur, as well as chronicle the wildlife I see along the way. If it is my intention to create a book about this eight-day trip, I'll need the recording to remind me of what I am experiencing so it isn't all forgotten by the time I return home. But something isn't working correctly on the machine. Then I notice a little switch that puts it on pause. Perfect. When I pull off the road, I can quickly pick up the recorder from the passenger seat, click the record button, and talk for a few minutes about what I've been seeing. Click stop. Set it back down on the seat beside me. Resume travel.

Blackberries are growing wild by the freeway and at times growing in the median as well. They are flourishing and are loaded with white blossoms. The grasses beside the freeway are high in places that haven't already been mowed. Buttercups are now visible everywhere as the dandelion season has come and gone.

I try exit 109, Yale Road West, near the golf course just west of Chilliwack. I take some pictures of the golf course and mountains to the south. The lighting isn't good, and I can see the pictures will not do the area justice. Then I continue on to Chilliwack.

Exit 116, Lickman Road, in Chilliwack. This is a planned stop. I'll pick up a tea at the McDonalds and go on to Hofstede's to buy a favourite sandwich of mine—a turkey, apple, curry panini with brie. A quick detour first down a side road where I get a picture of an old barn. Old barns are not typical structures in this area. I just happen to like the character of them. Again, I'm disappointed with the lighting. It's the wrong time of day for a good picture from this angle. I also get a picture of a field planted with corn, now several inches high. The Chilliwack area is known for corn, in particular a variety known as peaches and cream—tender and sweet.

Old barn near Chilliwack

Corn field near Chilliwack

I drive up to the McDonalds and am shocked. The sign says closed for renovations, but heavy machinery works around a pile of rubble. The entire building has been demolished. My cousin who passed away several years ago built this particular McDonalds. I feel an odd sort of loss with it now gone and slightly guilty I was unaware it was being torn down. It makes me wonder what else has happened that I don't know about.

Perhaps I've had enough tea this morning. I can get one later in Merritt. Hofstede's is busy and I'm forced to choose between waiting in a lineup, all of us masked and six feet apart, and missing out on my panini. I choose to wait despite feeling impatient. The sandwiches are that good! I plan to eat it as I make my recording/photo stops.

After Chilliwack, the valley with all its lush farmland begins to narrow and the mountains are closer to the road.

Panini from Hofstede's in Chilliwack

Fraser Valley farmland

I get glimpses of the Fraser River on my left. Soon rain begins to sprinkle on my windshield. The clouds have gathered overhead, blocking out the blue sky. There is a good breeze blowing. I'm getting closer to the town of Hope and the mountains get closer still. Clouds bump into them, dropping moisture, but I'm used to encountering rain in this area. I bypass Hope, a little community of around six thousand situated where the end of the Fraser Valley meets the southern end of the Fraser Canyon. Hope is surrounded by mountains. I catch glimpses of the town off to my left as the highway climbs before I turn onto Highway 5, or the Coquihalla Highway as it is also known.

From Hope to Merritt, B.C.

It is 110 kilometres from Hope to Merritt, my next stop. This road travels through wilderness. No little laneways into someone's home, no gas stations, no traffic lights. This is over one hundred kilometres of nothing but tree-covered mountains and the highway cutting its way over and around the mountains, part of the North Cascades range. It begins at sea level in Hope, then gains one kilometre in elevation over the next fifty kilometres of roadway. There are a lot of hills ahead to climb.

As the road gains in elevation, I leave summer behind. Although technically we are not in summer yet, back home in Surrey it felt like summer. My rose bushes were in full bloom. My flower containers overflowed with petunias, alyssum, geraniums, sweet peas, and other blossoming plants. My lawn has been mowed every two weeks since early April. My lilac bush was at its best weeks earlier and all the lovely fragrant blossoms are now just a memory. But here, along the "Coq," grasses are getting shorter and sparser as the road climbs. As I near the highest elevation, mountains are still streaked with snow and the bushes at the roadside are just now showing the first signs of greening. Spring has barely arrived here.

So far today I've seen no wildlife on this section of the highway, nor did I expect to. Over the years, I've seen only a couple of deer and just once a black bear meandering along a river. Deer are more likely to be found in a farmer's field or in a clearing in the forest. Along a highway with rock-faced cliffs and steep mountains heavily treed with evergreens, there isn't much vegetation to attract deer near the roadside. Also, they tend to come out into the open near dawn and nightfall.

It has been overcast through the mountains and now, at the summit, fog obscures the top. I had hoped to have a nice picture of the summit with its sheer rock face but that is not the picture available today. I settle for a mountain shot close to the summit and a frame showing some of the rock and snow at the highest point.

Coquihalla Highway nearing the summit

Since this book is about capturing my experiences over an eight-day period, it's likely some of the pictures will be taken in overcast or rainy conditions. It's unfortunate, but part of the adventure of life is learning to accept the less-than-perfect moments too. And so, the best I can do is tell you that sometimes the summit is spectacular. I've seen the rock face after a rain, sunlight highlighting its features. I've seen it in the winter loaded down with snow sparkling in the sunshine. It feels special to see it at its best. Yet, today it is shrouded with cloud and sits gloomily as if being 4,081 feet above sea level is nothing to cheer about.

Summit—top obscured by cloud

The speed limit for the Coquihalla Highway is 120 km/h for most of the route. It varies from four to six lanes so it is generally easy highway driving. Today I'm trying to see everything as if for the first time and record my impressions.

Friends find driving stressful. I find it relaxing, a time of renewal. I seldom have the radio on while I drive as I don't want my attention divided. I like the silence inside a car, with just the sound of the tires on the highway. I'm not trying to "make good time" or reach a destination by a specific hour. My intention is to spot any wildlife that might come near the road as I'm passing and to notice particularly beautiful scenery. Because either could occur at any time, I prefer no traffic behind me so I can have ample time to respond, either by stopping or backing up if necessary.

There's a rest stop just past the summit, and I see a number of police cars on the other side of the road. Because of the Covid restrictions, they are checking travellers heading for the lower mainland.

There is no police road check on my side of the highway, so I do not have to offer my carefully prepared explanation. I'm thankful for my rental property as an excuse, but I do plan on getting as much enjoyment out of this trip as possible. My spirit is badly in need of renewal. I think of those families who have spent the entire winter in their small bubble isolating from others. What harm could come from a family renting a cabin and letting their kids swim in a lake or hike trails? We have had months and months of fear aimed at us, daily death counts on every TV station. I find the whole situation oppressive and am thankful for the seeming freedom of being on the open highway.

Soon after the summit, I notice the sky is starting to open up. The grass at the side of the road is more plentiful and is about two inches high. The trees here are all fully in leaf.

I start the long climb up Larson Hill, then down the other side, across the valley floor, and up the other side. The skies are very blue right now. It's at this point on the highway, crossing this divide, I know Merritt will soon come into sight.

When I find a wider shoulder as I get closer to Merritt, I take the opportunity to pull over for several pictures. I love this area—coming down into the Nicola Valley. The clouds are casting shadows on the mountains and hillsides. Rolling hills look like great lumps of bread dough, giant finger indents on the sides where grasses grow thicker or trees find a place to take root. The scenery here always makes me long to paint. It seems there is no way to capture the ambiance with a camera, so perhaps on a canvas. I wonder if others coming down this immense curving highway with the Nicola Valley spread out below feel captivated by creative longings they will probably never fulfill. There is something almost magical about this place, casting its spell over me, demanding I respond to its beauty.

Coquihalla Hwy nearing Merritt, B.C.

I stop in Merritt for a tea at McDonalds and a bathroom break, then cross the road to top up my gas tank. Merritt has grown a lot in the past years. It used to feel like a dusty, dingy little community, but now it is thriving with a population of around seven thousand people. I believe the Merritt Mountain Music Festival has helped put it on the map, attracting many country music stars for the annual event. Plans are already underway for life after Covid—the 2022 season now named the Rockin' River Music Fest.

From Merritt to Sun Peaks, just north of Kamloops, B.C.

There are decisions to be made. Highway 5 will take me from Merritt to Kamloops in just seventy-nine kilometres. Highway 5A will also get me to Kamloops but the drive is longer—ninety-two kilometres of winding road. At 3:45 in the afternoon, I decide to take the longer route on 5A. I've driven this road before and love the pastoral scenes. It's worth the extra time. And I might spot some deer or a coyote. I'm anxious to record any sightings. I love that moment of spotting wildlife in its natural setting. The delight never lessens.

Highway 5A passes on the east side of Nicola Lake, a curving body of water approximately twenty-two kilometres long. In the past, I have seen Nicola Lake when it has been so still, so mirror-like, that it reflected the entire surrounding hills and cloud formations on its surface. Today the water is rough and a dense dark blue in colour. Apparently, there are over twenty species of fish in the lake. Good to know if I should ever decide to trade my camera in for a fishing pole. Today is all about the camera though.

Nicola Lake

The lake is rimmed with last year's grasses, tall and white. There are weeping willows further along in spring green. The wind is blowing like crazy. I rest my elbows on my car roof to steady the camera. The colours are fresh and vibrant, and at the same time there are subtle shades of greens and beiges. As I travel the highway, I take a ridiculous number of photos, alternating between my camera and my cell phone.

Sheep grazing in the field along Hwy 5A

I have been captivated by this stretch of highway in the past. It's like I have stumbled into a time zone, or even a different dimension, where everything moves slowly. The light is perfect today. Everything is enhanced. The colours in the sky call out for my attention. I wonder how I will decide which pictures to use for this book as I have taken so many. Now it is five o'clock and Kamloops is still fifty kilometres away.

Countryside along Hwy 5A

There are cows grazing in pastures, an old, abandoned building or two, and several smaller lakes, each with their own charm. The sky and reflected light, hillsides draped with shadows from drifting clouds, there is too much to see and take in. I don't want to miss any of the images that present themselves to me over and over.

Field and hillside along Hwy 5A

Lake and hills along Hwy 5A

Because the landscape is quite open compared to the mountainous and heavily treed terrain I drove through earlier today, the contours of the land adds to the spell I am under. I am smitten! I tell my tape recorder this might be the most beautiful ninety-two kilometres of roadway that I know of. I text an artist friend and tell him he must, must, must come for a drive along here on a sunny day while little, fleece-like clouds move overhead. "Bring your camera," I add.

Huge rock in field along Hwy 5A

Now it is 5:38 and Kamloops is still, at minimum, a half an hour away. It has taken me thirty-eight minutes to travel fifteen kilometres. Ridiculous, but the scenery is so stunning I can't help it. I feel half intoxicated with the light and shadows on the hillsides, with the first blush of greenery on the fields, of the sunlight on the stubble from last year's crops, the dark, rich brown of a plowed field.

Lake with storm clouds in the distance along Hwy 5A

I continue to take pictures, stopping every time a scene draws my attention.

Farmland with rain falling in the distance, Hwy 5A

    I can see it is raining up ahead. Then I'm in the midst of it. The skies open up and a downpour ensues. I turn on my windshield wipers and pick up my pace. I am grateful for the interruption. Otherwise, I might never reach my destination tonight.

I take the most direct route through Kamloops, continuing on Hwy 5 north for fifteen minutes until I exit at Heffley Creek and onto Tod Mountain Road.

I'm staying at a timeshare in Sun Peaks, a ski community about fifty-six kilometres north of Kamloops. On the way up the hill off the main highway, I see the only animal I've seen all day—a fat, squat marmot by the side of the road. A sigh of disappointment—no time to stop and take a picture. Check-in time is between 4 and 7 p.m. I arrive with only three minutes to spare.

As I fill out the required paperwork, the clerk mentions that five people scheduled to arrive haven't showed up. He thinks it's probably due to Covid restrictions as they were from Alberta. Meaning it as a joke, I say, "So you're telling me I'm the only person staying at the Lodge."

"Yes," he replies, much to my shock. "And in the morning for your complimentary breakfast, I'll be serving fruit with yogurt, followed by eggs benedict. Will that be suitable?"

It seems a preposterous situation—to be the only guest. I decide to enjoy this once-in-a-lifetime experience of feeling like a queen for a day.

"That will be lovely," I say, hopefully with a regal tone.

Today's Recap

Sightings: .... Marmot

Most memorable moments: .... The scenery on Highway 5A

DAY TWO –
Sunday, June 6, 2021

Sun Peaks to Valemount, B.C.

WHEN I COME DOWNSTAIRS INTO the dining room, two young men are already there. They must have been late arrivals. I choose a table at least twelve feet away. My breakfast is served and everything is lovely. The check-in clerk from the previous night, carefully masked, is our chef this morning. I soon discover that he found the young men sleeping in their car outside and invited them in for breakfast as the food had already been purchased for the guests who didn't show. What an unusual gesture of generousity! Soon all four of us are in conversation, although at a distance. One man is from England and his friend is from Australia. They are touring British Columbia. We talk about their plans and possible routes. I'm taken back in memory to my visits of both England and Australia. The atmosphere in the dining room seems charged with anticipation. If I was from the other side of the world and had only this day to see B.C., what would that be like? One chance, just once chance to absorb as much as possible. It's a perspective I try to carry with me for the rest of the day.

    It's 10 a.m. by the time I've finished breakfast and loaded the car. My odometer reads 159,412. It's a cool day with blue skies and fluffy white clouds as I come down Tod Mountain Road. Dandelions by the roadside have gone to seed. Lilac bushes, in full blossom and in various shades of purple, decorate some properties. I casually consider the possibility of breaking off a small bouquet from a bush near the road so my car will be filled with the scent, one of my favourites. No, too out of character. But what if I simply walk to the edge of the lawn and deeply breathe in the fragrance? Much as I might like to, that also remains outside my comfort zone. I drive on. Wild roses are blooming beside the road. I don't stop to smell them either.

At one point, I see a billboard showing a picture of a missing young man, Ryan. I noticed it on my way up last night and was reminded of being here two years earlier with my teenaged granddaughter. She and I saw a woman walking along the roadside stopping to look over the embankment. We guessed she was looking for her dog or had lost something so stopped to ask if we could help. It was then we heard her heartbreaking story. Her son had been up at Sun Peaks months earlier. The last time he was seen was going out for a walk. The anguish of this poor mother seemed unbearable—to continue to walk the road looking for signs when it all seemed quite hopeless. We drove on, unable to comfort her or help in any way. This billboard shows that she is still trying two years later, against hope, to locate her son. I'm not sure how someone can bear the pain when there is no closure.

Billboard on Tod Mountain

As I continue down the mountain, I take more photos. It is going to be a beautiful day. I wonder, at what point are people able to see beauty again after the darkness of grief?

Scene from Tod Mountain Road

I like to take pictures of pastoral scenes. But I also enjoy the sunlight dancing through the leaves, golden flashes, and the appearance of the sandy cliffs on the other side of the road. There are a variety of species of trees here. Brown hillsides, trees casting shadows. I don't stop to take pictures. There are too many possible choices. I will have to leave this world some day without fully appreciating all the beauty. There is simply too much. My eyes fill with tears and I am uncertain if I'm moved by the overwhelming amount of beauty in our world or if I'm just feeling heartsick for Ryan's mother. Perhaps both.

Scene from Tod Mountain

At Heffley Creek, I turn right onto Hwy 5 north heading for Barriere. The terrain is quite open here. The road is elevated above the valley floor. I can see the North Thompson River below and farmlands spread out along it. There are mountains, or at least very high hills, on either side of the valley. Pictureque. My type of scenery. I am ever alert to the possibility of wildlife.

I feel disheartened by the power lines and power poles, because no matter where I look, they are there. I try to erase them from my mind because they really disturb the overall ambience. I like new subdivisions with their underground wiring. In the countryside, I realize, it is not practical. Just interesting to note that our surroundings would be even more beautiful if not marred by transformers, power poles, and heavy black cables.

At this moment, the sun is bringing out the best in the landscape. It is a stellar day.

Looking at our traffic and judging it from all appearances, I'd say most people think our purpose is to get from one place to another. And, to be sure, there are many times when I do just that. I have to get groceries. I go to work. I have to pick up something from my daughter's place. But no matter what our daily chores involve, I'll offer the proposition that perceiving and appreciating the beauty around us is even more important. Today is unique in its visuals. It will never again be here in exactly the same way, and it is pretty spectacular. I cannot take it all in. I stop at the side of the road to take a picture of the

Field between Heffley Creek and Barriere

clouds and a pile of rocks in a field. Nothing can grow on rocks and the farmer likely wishes they weren't there, but I like how it looks. I cannot explain why, but I do. When everything is more or less right with the world, meaning all my family and friends are healthy and reasonably happy and I have time to experience the landscape in a leisurely way, like today, then I am filled, overwhelmed, with joy. I do mean joy, but I am searching in my mind for a different word. Joy feels overused, or misused. I need a word that means "all is well with the world despite everything that is not well with the world." I'm filled with a deep contentment—a sense of wellbeing, a sense of joy. I'll have to check my thesaurus at home.

The hills in this region remind me of a teenaged boy growing a beard. There are random trees here and there on the slopes, rather like the stubble and sparse growth on a teen's face.

I want to take a picture but there is no place to pull off the road, so I'll have to describe it. The highway rounds a corner and there is a big rock cliff across the road from me. Bubbling up behind the cliff are large white clouds and the nicest blue sky. Sun highlights the new grass, turning it a vibrant shade of green. Shadows from other clouds are draped over the hillside here and there. I try to inhale it, to absorb it. It seems a shame that I have no way of retaining and reviewing this scene in my memory. But worse still is to be one of these people today in too much of a hurry to notice this at all.

The hillsides are changing. Now many have downed trees or blackened dead poles reaching into the sky, remnants of a forest fire in 2003.

I'm taking a lot of pictures: an old barn with a wooden fence, the contours of a plowed field. But I am seeing no animals. That was to be the main focus of the book—to list wild animals I would see from the roadside. I find it very exciting to spot an animal in its natural setting and I am assuming that others would be intrigued with that possibility. And so far, nothing. With the way the sunlight is enhancing the landscape yesterday and today, the scenery has been awesome. But will that be enough to spell adventure to readers?

After I pass through Barriere, a little community of 1,700 people, I eventually come to a place on the highway that is special to me. Immediately beyond a curve, there is a derelict barn and house on a flat piece of farmland just barely higher than the North Thompson River that is flowing by. I've been flirting with this spot for years. I've squeezed onto the shoulder and prayed no big transport trucks came thundering by as I stood by my car taking pictures of the buildings, their weathered exteriors appearing silver in the sunlight. In the summer when the water is lower, I've seen eagles out on a sand bar fishing. I've thought many times of trying to find out who owns it and whether it is for sale. There is no "For Sale" sign but then again, there is no indication that anyone is harvesting the fields either. It does not seem to be a safe place to build, being so close to the river and on such low ground, but my imagination is captivated by thoughts of spending a few weekends here each year, relaxing, watching the water flow by. I can imagine my children and grandchildren arriving, playing catch in the field, and fishing on the banks of the river. At my age, it is unlikely that I will ever pursue this, even if there was an opportunity. Still, dreams are fun.

Burned out area from 2003

There is no one behind me as I approach the corner, and I suddenly realize there is an old driveway I've never noticed before. I quickly signal (an automatic reflex) and pull off into the incredibly overgrown drive.

Overgrown driveway to abandoned farm

I get out and eye the pathway suspiciously . The narrow wheel tracks are free from vegetation but weeds, knee deep, encroach upon it. Snakes! That's my worry! Deep breath. Do I risk it—all for the sake of a picture? I walk along the path cautiously. A butterfly zigzags lazily up from some wildflowers, and I try to remember the last time I saw a butterfly in Surrey. More steps. Finally, the old barn comes into view. The sun is almost directly overhead and isn't helpful with the lighting. I take a few pictures and return to my car as slowly and carefully as I came.

Abandoned farm

Safely back in the car, I congratulate myself for my bravery. I realize it was a very tiny display of bravery, but still!

It is important in life not to be more afraid than is necessary. Equally important, we should not be less afraid than necessary. Friends sometimes comment on my courage, meaning I do things they would not dream of doing. This trip would be a good example. They misunderstand, however. It has taken no courage to plan and anticipate such a trip. That was just fun. I consider myself a cautious adventurer. I dislike how fear can rob a person of many joys. It's important to put risks into perspective. For example, everytime we leave our homes, there is the risk of a motor vehicle accident. Even if we are walking, a car could go out of control and hit us. But because it is such a common risk, we tend to compensate for it and don't quake with fear as we step outside. When we consider something less common, like going on a four thousand kilometre road trip, our worries can magnify. The "what ifs" can overtake our common sense and prevent us from having wonderful experiences. So, I repeat, it is important not to be more afraid than is necessary.

The road leads to a higher elevation and hugs the hillside at the edge of what seems to be a flood plain. There are farms with standing water in places. Has the river overflowed not long ago or is the ground too saturated to absorb a recent rain?

Flooded land between Barriere and Little Fort

On the other side of the river, the mountains have rocky outcroppings. I stop to take pictures of six horses in a field. While outside the car, I notice eagles high above the road, drifting in the sunlight. It's futile to try to get a good picture with my little camera. It's simply not powerful enough. Of course I try anyway.

Two eagles, mere specks in the sky

Little Fort is in the North Thompson Valley region known as High Country. The North Thompson River often looks, as it does today, in danger of overflowing. Little Fort has a population of 350 people. I've stopped at the gas station a few times in the past on my way through. Just across the road from the gas station is a cattle farm. I like to take several pictures of the cows and their calves. Cows are strange creatures. I say this even after living on a farm as a child. Back then, I was quite frightened of them. When I pull off to the side of the road, they notice. Not only do they notice, but they seem curious and start to move towards me. Slow swaying bodies, tilt of the head, big cow eyes wanting to know what's going on. It makes me want to visit for awhile or say something profound to reward them for ambling over to the fence that separates us. Instead, I admire their offspring and take a few pictures.

Cows at Little Fort

When I get to Clearwater, I stop at the tourist bureau. The road to my left will take me into Wells Grey Provincial Park. The park covers over five thousand square kilometres and protects the wilderness of much of the Cariboo Mountains.

There was a particularly grizzly murder in the park years ago when my children were young, so I was somewhat influenced by that memory and have never ventured into the park. I ask the tourist bureau staff member about taking a short drive in that direction and she points out on a map one of the nearest attractions, a waterfall near the road. The roadside into the park is densely treed and about all I can see are trees.

I endure and cross over into the provincial park lands. There, I've overcome my reluctance to go into Wells Grey Park! Minutes later, I decide not to give much time to this detour and return to Hwy 5 north.

On the Yellowhead Hwy, rain in the distance

This section of the highway is also known as the Yellowhead Highway. Doesn't that name seem to spell adventure? I love the romance of place names and highway names. Who wouldn't want to travel on the Yellowhead Highway? I think of past trips along this route. I once saw a large black bear feeding on vegetation by the roadside. And on another trip, I saw a young moose beside the stream quite far from the road. It stood and looked at me with curiosity in much the same way cows seem to. However, it never ambled over to see what I was doing, so I was left with pictures too far away to be much good.

At 1:50 in the afternoon, it begins to rain. Valemount, my destination for this evening, is still 215 kilometres away. But I see lots of blue sky up ahead. And then it starts to rain heavily. No more pictures at the moment. The river, when I can get glimpses of it, is choppy. Wild. Scary.

Eventually, it stops raining, and I'm a lot closer to Valemount, only 140 kilometres to go. There is a big mountain behind me but the top is fogged in. I'm on high alert for bear or moose, as sightings of either are possible here. But nothing.

The sun comes out and brightens up the world.

Wildflowers

Wildflowers

Then rain. I look up and it feels confusing. I can see blue patches among the clouds but the clouds don't look dark enough to hold rain. Yet I keep encountering these intermittant showers.

Nesting swan

Somewhere between Clearwater and Blue River, I see two swans in what appears to be a very shallow pond. They are too far away for me to get a decent picture. I'm a little disappointed that so far my only sightings are these swans.

Scenery nearing Valemount

I drive into Valemount. The townsite and surrounding area are flat, circled by snow-topped mountain ranges. I find my hotel, put on my Covid mask, and check in. I touch the pen as I sign the form. I touch the button on the elevator door, all part of my awareness now. When I get into my room, I carefully and thoroughly wash my hands, put my frozen food in the fridge, then stretch out on the bed for a short nap.

Valemount to Jasper, AB and back to Valemount, B.C.

At 6:30 in the evening, I head out in the direction of the town of Jasper, Alberta. This is the same route I will take tomorrow morning so why would I drive it tonight? With some animals, you're more likely to see them in the early hours. With others, the evening is ideal. I decide to go out feeling certain my patience will be rewarded. Jasper is 124 kilometres away and lies within the Jasper National Park, an area of eleven thousand square kilometres. I have never failed to see wildlife in this area.

Mount Robson B.C. in the distance

First I pass through Mount Robson Park, which is still in British Columbia.

Catching a glimpse of a wild animal in its natural setting can make my day. If the animal stays around long enough for me to get a few pictures, then that is truly a plus. Animals show up when they show up. I have gone out into the countryside in the right season and at the optimum time of day (or evening) but have seen nothing. Another time, I'll be fortunate to see a number of animals. It's best to be prepared for disappointment, but to let your gratitude run wild if you should be so fortunate to see anything.

Several years ago, I watched two grizzles feast on a huge patch of dandelions in Jasper National Park, so I planned this trip hoping the dandelions would be in full bloom. My timing has worked out nicely. Spring comes much later to the interior and northern areas of the province, long after the yellow flashes of dandelions on lawns and in ditches in the lower mainland have disappeared. I've been unable to dislike the dandelions each spring since I discovered how much bears like them. I see their yellow heads popping up on my lawn and think, *bear season.*

Moose Lake

I stop at Moose Lake as I have many times. It's a huge lake, 11.7 kilometres long, and I'm always hoping to see a moose swimming across it. To date, I have never seen one in this area. Just east of Moose Lake is another body of water that appears quite shallow. It is usually very still and offers a wonderful reflection. I've often seen ducks and Canada geese paddling about on these waters.

Shallow water just east of Moose Lake

I drive the entire distance to Jasper knowing I'll see elk around the townsite because there are always elk in Jasper. The first elk I ever saw was grazing on the lawn outside a B&B home I was staying in. That was more than a little alarming. It was a very large elk and I slipped quietly into the safety of my car. Tonight—nothing!

Sunlight breaking through the clouds in the park

My focus is keen the entire drive from Jasper back to Valemount, certain at any moment I'll see an elk or at least a deer. The tricky part of spotting animals in the evening is that they prefer to stay out of sight until dusk, and then, of course, the poor lighting makes it difficult to take good pictures. No worries on that account this evening. I see nothing, not even a chipmunk. Nothing.

I feel crushed. I've considered doing a book like this for a number of years. Now that I'm actually doing it and recording my impressions—and I have the time available to take as many pictures as I want—I can't believe I'm seeing nothing.

Mountains in B.C. heading for Valemount

There is much beautiful scenery, however. I settle for a couple of pictures as my plan is to get plenty of scenery photos tomorrow.

Heading back to Valemount as evening falls

Sunset happened at 9:18 this evening and by the time I get back to my hotel in Valemount, it is raining slightly and almost totally dark.

I return to my room and text my daughters to let them know I am safely at my planned destination for the night. I gave my family copies of my itinery with the plan to check in each evening, a small nod to safety.

Today's Recap

Sightings: .... Two swans

Most memorable moments: .... The lighting in the first part of the day

DAY THREE –
Monday, June 7, 2021

Valemount, B.C. to Hinton, AB

IT SEEMED LIKE A GOOD idea to be on the road at dawn hoping for animal sightings, but when I checked on sunrise, I found out it happens at 4:37 a.m. Scrap that idea! I knew the days are longer in summer in the north but hadn't realized just how much longer.

By 7:12, I have checked out of the hotel and am in my car. The odometer reads 160,011. It is raining quite heavily. I shouldn't start out the day feeling disappointed, but I am. Perhaps the weather will clear shortly. Hard to tell around the mountains. I'll travel north on Hwy. 5 for about twenty kilometres, then turn right onto Hwy 16 east, also part of the Yellowhead Hwy. I'll be retracing the route I took last evening to Jasper. With better results, I hope.

I pull out onto the highway and up ahead see a dog standing at the edge of the road. My wipers are slapping out their beat, and my windshield is fogging up at the same time. I slow just in case the dog should run out in front of me and turn on my defrost trying to clear the window.

It's not a dog.

It's a young moose!

I need to do everything at once: pull off the road, grab my camera from the seat beside me, turn it on. Or is it better with my cell phone? Wipers push great plops of water off the windshield. Is it better to turn them off and take the picture through the rain or risk catching the wipers in motion? I am so excited, as well as annoyed by the rain ruining a great moment, that I can hardly get the camera turned on. I hit the button several times. Did it click? Did the picture take? I can't tell. A large transport truck comes toward us and in a blink of an eye, the moose turns and is gone.

Moose near rail overpass in Valemount, B.C.

It is about seventy-six kilometres from the turnoff onto Hwy 16 east until I reach the Alberta border. In the meantime, I drive beside stretches of the Fraser River. It is quite tame looking compared to the broad expanse of the Fraser River down at the coast. It is still raining when I enter Mount Robson Park. The park is 2,249 square kilometres in size. Mount Robson is massive, almost four thousand metres high. I can relate to distance in metres, but for something like the height of a mountain (or of people), I still feel more comfortable using the old measurements. In those terms, Mount Robson is over thirteen thousand feet high. Today, the top is obscured by cloud. I had hoped—of course I had hoped—for a clear day so I could show a dramatic picture of its splendor. It is not to be.

I stop at Moose Lake. At one end is a rest stop with an inviting place to park the car. From there, I can take pictures of the other end of the lake with the mountains for dramatic background. Today the mountains have been eliminated by clouds, just as surely as if they had been erased. I snap a photo just so I can compare it with the one I took last night. Every time I pass Moose Lake, I feel a surge of optimism in my heart. Perhaps I will see a moose this time. There are shallow bodies of water just beyond the lake where ducks and geese like to raise their young. It looks like an ideal stomping ground for a moose but, no, I've never spotted one in the area, although I've talked to others who have. Moose seem to be a most elusive species, which is why I was so excited to see the young moose earlier this morning.

This area of the country is spectacular. I'm used to the mountains around the lower mainland and after a length of time away from the Canadian Rockies, I begin to forget their true size. Then I will return to this area and—it has never failed—again be in awe of their impact. I've looked forward to taking pictures for this book, to show people just how immense these mountains are. But it's raining. No, it's really raining! The mountains have virtually disappeared. Occasionally, I get a glimpse of something out in the foggy distance but I cannot see it. What a turn of events this is!

Moose Lake, mountains obscured by cloud

I reach the Alberta border and the clock on my dashboard leaps ahead an hour. When I check in with the staff at the entrance to Jasper National Park, I mention the rain. The cheerful young woman says not to worry, the weather changes quickly. "It could clear at any time. It often does."

She sounded optimistic, even knowledgeable, but it doesn't clear. I have the highway in front of me and trees on either side of the road. This could be a rainy day anywhere. Nothing around me suggests that I'm travelling among spectacular mountains with majestic peaks. I did not anticipate the possibility of not seeing the Rockies as I drive through them. I'm into the third day of an eight-day trip and all I have for my book is a rainy, blurry picture of a moose. It would be silly to feel disappointed. There is no way to guarantee good weather, and animal sightings are always hit or miss. And yet disappointment sits in my chest like a heavy weight. I try reasoning with myself. If I don't have material for the book this time, there is always next year. I've told no one my plans so I don't have to be embarrassed when I fail to create a book. None of this encouraging self-talk dispels my disappointment or dampens my intention to share my travels with others. Finally, I start singing fragments of old camping songs just to change the mood. It's interesting how singing, even off-key and without all the words, can literally lift my spirits.

Finally, I exit Jasper National Park. It has rained the entire way. Soon I'm in Hinton. I make a dash through the rain into McDonalds for a bathroom stop and a cup of tea.

Hinton to Slave Lake

Back on the highway, I soon see one deer, and then another, each at a different spot, dead beside the road—victims of encounters with traffic. I shake my head in bewilderment. What kind of a trip is this?

I continue east on Hwy 16 towards Edmonton. Then the rain stops. It's a four-lane highway and the sky opens up ahead of me. There is not very much traffic. The landscape seems friendlier than before. Now that's an odd observation. What is it, I wonder, that makes me feel this way? I decide it is because there are more deciduous trees in the mix now. Do broad-leafed trees seem friendlier to others than evergreens? They are often used to create borders around farmland. I suppose a pastoral scene is more welcoming than a forest.

Farmland in Alberta

Up ahead, I see a broad sheet of grey coming down from the sky. I know that when I reach that point on the landscape, I will experience heavy rain once more. Overhead are some big dark clouds interspersed with open patches, light breaking through. The south is more open with smaller white clouds. This sense of an immense skyscape is something I love about Alberta. There is as much to see overhead as there is in the landscape. Far to the north there is blue sky. A good omen, for eventually I will make my way in that direction.

I pull off the highway, take a quick look at my roadmap, and make an instant decision. I will take Hwy 32 to Whitecourt. For those of you who have never tried it, this is one of the advantages of travelling alone—instant decisions and no recriminations.

I stop in Whitecourt at another McDonalds for more tea and a cold bottle of water. The cooler in my trunk has enough food for at least another day, so I'm not yet concerned about purchasing food.

Next I turn east onto Hwy 658. This is a smaller road, paved, but just two-way traffic. Trees come right up to the edge of the road. There isn't much of a shoulder. Just before the community of Blue Ridge, a deer runs across the road in front of me and into the woods on the other side. No time to get a picture. But still, I am elated. This is progress.

Then, up ahead, a young black bear emerges from the trees on the opposite side of the road. I slow down and pull off to the side, but it runs back into the bush before I can reach my camera. I drive along the pavement for a bit, make a U-turn, and slowly come back hoping I'll spot it again. But nothing. As I turn around to continue on my way, I notice an adult black bear among low bushes in a field not far away. I'm assuming this is the mother of the young bear I saw minutes earlier. As I slow to a stop, she runs into the heavier underbrush. Again, no picture. It's one thing to report on animal sightings. It's another to present proof. I have the sinking feeling that this is like describing the fish that got away. Never a convincing story. But so far, Hwy 658 is showing promise.

Eventually, I meet up with Hwy 33, which has been my intention for months now. I can no longer remember where I heard about this road, nicknamed the Grizzly Highway, but my mind instantly grasped onto it and wouldn't let go. I talked with a co-worker who had travelled to northern areas of Alberta. Was he familiar with Hwy 33?

"Yes," he said. "You have to be careful because of the amount of wildlife along there, but it's a decent road."

I'm sure he had no idea I consider wildlife a plus, not something to be cautioned against. So Hwy 33 became my new dream, and I poured over the map figuring out how I could work this into my trip to Chetwynd. It is far enough away from my destination as to make the concept humorous. Clearly, gathering material for my book and the adventure of seeing new territory comes before any consideration of checking on my property.

Hwy 33 runs from Hwy 43 near Gunn (close to Edmonton) and takes a north-west path ending at Hwy 2 near Kinuso in the vicinity of Lesser Slave Lake. I was meeting up with Hwy 33 part way along its path. My problem now was that I wanted to drive this section of highway in the evening, a time when I might see more animals, but it's only 3:30 in the afternoon. I will only get to do this once. I might as well do it right. So I chose to go south, in the opposite direction, a route I will backtrack after dinner tonight.

I continue in this southerly direction until I reach Barrhead, a good sized town of just under five thousand people. I drive into an A&W and wonder what their Covid guidelines are. Will I be allowed inside? I put on my mask and pull on the door. It opens. Thankfully, I am able to use their facilities. I order a teen burger, my first purchased food of this trip, a bottle of water, and more tea. It's still not time to begin my drive north, and I'm aware I'm tired. It was an early start today and I've driven many kilometres. I move my car as far from the drive-thru as I can and decide on a nap. I once read that it's important to do certain things if you decide to sleep in a car so that a tired mind will never associate the normal driving position with sleep. I undo my seat belt, move my seat as far back as possible so I can stretch my legs, and recline the seat. I've already locked my car doors and turned the windows down a crack. I set the timer on my cell phone and scrunch around to get as comfortable as possible. Then I fall asleep.

When the alarm goes off, I feel surprisingly refreshed. I reposition the seat, take a big drink of cold water, and set out to "do" the Grizzly Highway. I am optimistic, a little, but it's still so bright out. It's not even close to being dusk. But it's 180 kilometres from Barrhead to Kinuso and another thirty kilometres into Slave Lake where I have reservations for the night. And if I stop to take many pictures . . .

I start out. In a very short time, a deer crosses the road in front of me. I pull over, grab my camera . . . and it's gone. I think of all the wildlife pictures I have on my computer. Hundreds! Why is it I can't seem to get a picture of anything on this trip?

A rain cloud finds me, and for the next while I'm looking through raindrops and windshield wipers. I do a slight detour into Fort Assiniboine, just because it's there. I've never found a place that I wouldn't like to visit for at least a few minutes. There's a certain affinity I have with place names. They stick in my head and they remain as places I've never been. It's rather like knowing you have a first cousin you've never met who lives in Austin, Texas. So, if you're anywhere near Austin at some point in your life, you might just decide to look her up. It's like that for me and place names.

Fort Assiniboine Museum and Friendship Club

I drive into Fort Assiniboine, look around, take a few pictures, and leave feeling quite satisfied I've accomplished at least a short meeting. It would have been almost rude to be so close and not become slightly acquainted. I drive over a bridge. The sign says it's the Athabasca River. I feel extraordinarily pleased. I hadn't known I would be seeing the Athabasca River. Friends pour over brochures of cruises and talk of buffet tables and days of relaxation. Not me. I get excited by visiting Fort Assiniboine and seeing the Athabasca River. I hear about the highway opened up to Tuktoyaktuk and dream of finding someone who would do that journey with me, north to the edge of the Beauford Sea. An adventure of that sort is beyond my comfort zone as a single traveller, an example of a proper level of fear, in my opinion. But that is my idea of an amazing trip. I'd take hot dogs cooked by the side of the road over a buffet table on a cruise any day.

I pass through Swan Hills, a community of around 1,300 people. Another place I've never seen before.

Alberta countryside

The sky is now dark with clouds, like a thick mat overhead. It looks like nightfall is imminent. So when there is a break allowing the sun to shine through, I'm surprised it is still so high in the sky. Trees are close to the edge of the road on one side. On the other is a wider shoulder and then trees, so at this point all I'm seeing is dense forest. This continues kilometre upon kilometre upon kilometre. It feels like I've left civilization far behind. Yet it is not without enjoyment. I have never been here before, and it is unlikely I will ever be here again. So it's a once-in-a-lifetime experience, an opportunity I appreciate.

At one time in my life, I would have been bored by seeing so many trees, especially without the relief of any occasional field or pond. I used to consider trees simply as part of the background of my life. Ordinary and boring. Then one lazy weekend morning as I was avoiding getting up, my thoughts wandered to springtime and the ornamental cherry trees around the lower mainland. For some strange reason, I started wondering what it would be like to be a cherry tree, always in the same spot, just standing in the sunshine. And I thought about its roots bringing in water and minerals. Strange, although I've seen trees since I was born, this was the first time I ever wondered how a tree can make entirely different things, like bark and leaves, from the same ingredients. And how does it happen? Then I really thought about cherry blossoms and how they seem to push out through the bark. Something as fragile as a blossom starts as a bud but each delicate petal continues to grow as it opens. I know the information for all this is carried within the DNA of the tree, but suddenly the whole process seemed amazing.

Once I started thinking about the information stored in seeds, enough to begin a new tree, I was awe struck. And I'm still in that frame of mind. Which helps, I suppose, when I'm driving for so long seeing nothing but trees because I find it impossible to feel bored.

I find the self-confidence of trees inspiring. They sprout and then do their utmost to be the tree they are capable of being. An aspen tree doesn't feel badly about itself because it isn't a birch. A huge fir doesn't apologize for growing so tall and using more than its share of nutrients. We humans, on the other hand, seem to find it challenging to fully become our true selves.

As I get closer to the end of Hwy 33, fields and driveways become part of the landscape. I don't know why, but I am surprised. This seems unexpected. Lilacs are in bloom. The landscape is opening into nice farm country.

Early dusk

At the junction of Hwy 2, I turn right onto an amazingly smooth highway. This is such luxury after the road I've been on, but it doesn't last for long. I see Lesser Slave Lake off to my left and am surprised at how big the lake must be. I'm still a long way from the town of Slave Lake. So many dead trees around, remnants of an old forest fire, I assume.

I see a deer.

I see another deer and get a picture this time.

Deer by the road outside of Slave Lake, AB

Now I see three more deer and get pictures as well. They were all moving, so I'm not hopeful about clarity.

I check into a nice looking hotel at 9:10 in the evening. I can't see the lake from the hotel so I ask the clerk for directions. He points out that it's across the highway, down the road, and then I'm to follow the signs for the beach.

Just as the clerk said, I find the sign for the beach, continue along to the park, and eventually come to a long set of sturdy wooden stairs down to the beach. I can see through the thick trees that the sun seems to be setting but I can't get a clear picture from up here. I'm struggling with my own rules for safety. Rule number one: Don't leave paved roads. But to get here, I'm already on a dirt road, which seemed safe enough. Now, though, I have to get out of my car, with dusk approaching, and climb down a set of stairs to the beach. Rule number two: Don't do silly things like this. I rationalize that I don't hear voices in the distance. I don't see any other vehicles. It's Monday night. Decision—okay, but quickly. There is a solid flight of wooden stairs, a landing, then another flight of stairs down to the beach. Bushes block my view so I have to walk on the sand to get beyond the foilage. With each step, I sink about an inch into the sand. My shoes will be filled! I wonder how I could run in this should a bear suddenly appear. And then, there it is, a huge lake stretching off into the distance and rays of sunlight shooting down below the blanket of dark clouds. Quite spectacular. I push my apprehension down with the excitement of standing on the banks of Lesser Slave Lake just at sunset. I hadn't anticipated this part, had never even considered it a possibility, and I'm thrilled at the timing. It's easy to imagine how explorers might have felt seeing this lake for the first time.

I take my photographs, then start the long climb back up the stairway. Still no other cars in the parking lot. I empty my shoes, jump in the car, lock the doors, and breathe a sign of relief that this little excapade turned out okay. I won't have to explain to my family how I got robbed in a secluded spot or got attacked by a bear while wandering about in the underbrush all by myself.

Lesser Slave Lake nearing sunset

I drive through the park in a northerly direction watching for a break in the trees where I might get more pictures. When I feel I've exhausted all possibilities, I leave the park.

Nearing sunset on Lesser Slave Lake

I'm sure normal people, after a long day's drive, would go back to their hotel room and have a soak in the tub or watch TV. When adventure calls, some of us decide to "go for a little drive" out of town in the opposite direction just in case more animals are out and about. Which is what I do. I make bargains with myself. Just a few more kilometres and, if I don't see any animals, I'll turn around and go back to the hotel. A little bit longer. Just up and around the next hill. But nothing, so finally I turn around and head back. And then—I can see the sky glowing between the trees.

As I head back into town, the colour continues to seep and spread across the sky. That thick blanket of cloud overhead is now being lighted from underneath by the rays of the setting sun. Rose colours, purples, dark blues, spread out overhead in the most breathtaking way. I cannot believe my good fortune at being able to experience this. All tiredness has left my body. I feel wide-eyed with wonder.

I once spent a year taking pictures of a great many sunsets, and I remember how the impact of the sunset depended on the cloud cover, light bouncing off the various surfaces. Perhaps in the north sunsets have longer durations, I'm not sure. I'm only certain this is the most spectacular sunset I've ever seen. I pull off the road multiple times, taking pictures with both my camera and my cell phone. No matter the image in my viewfinder, I'm aware that the colour radiates over a much larger

Sunset near Slave Lake

area in all directions. It is impossible to really capture what I'm seeing. Finally, I get back to the hotel, satiated with beauty. Nevermind the lack of animal photos. Who could ask for more than what I have just experienced?

Sunset near Slave Lake

In the hotel parking lot, a man is taking a suitcase from the trunk of his car. "Did you see that sunset?" I ask.

He looks up. "No, why?"

I tell him he missed quite a sight. I ask the desk clerk the same question. He had missed it too.

I've noticed that when people return from vacations to exotic places, they often have the most amazing pictures of sunsets. I used to think it was the location that made them beautiful until I realized that our routines often interfere with us taking time to watch a sunset. They happen every day no matter where we are in the world. Mostly we just miss them.

Whenever I've gone out with my camera, intending to photograph the sunset, I find I return home changed by the experience. There is a stillness in the air as the sun falls below the horizon. No matter what kind of sky (except complete cloud and/or rain), there is immense beauty at this time of day. To be outside, to stand on the Earth being aware of its rotation for these few minutes, to be aware of the immense distance from the sun, to realize that our ancestors experienced this same phenomenon day after day, there is something terribly profound about being outside at sunset. Sometimes subtle colours, not much stronger than a whisper of orange on the horizon, at other times, such colours that make my heart race trying to capture them with my camera. Bold streaks of rose, edges of gold, light beams fanning out as the sun disappears moment by moment over what appears to be the edge of all that is. Subtle colours reverberating across the sky. Birds making their way to roost for the night. Pictures to challenge any vacation paradise photos.

Today's Recap

Animal sightings: ....Young moose

Deer – four individual sightings, one group of three

Black bear – two individual sightings (one juvenile, one adult)

Most memorable moments: .... Amazing sunset over Lesser Slave Lake

DAY FOUR –
Tuesday, June 8, 2021

Slave Lake to Peace River, AB

IT'S 6:44 IN THE MORNING as I load up my car. My odometer reads 160,828. It is four degrees outside and the windshield is covered with dew. Sunrise was at 4:59 a.m. or 3:59 a.m. B.C. time as Alberta is an hour ahead of B.C. The sun has already climbed a third of the way up the sky, so it feels like I'm getting a late start to the day.

It's interesting what different people like. Who would have thought I'd find it a great adventure to stand on the shore of Lesser Slave Lake at sunset? But it was. I felt connected back in time to all others who had done the same. I checked online for a few minutes last evening and found out that the lake is over one hundred kilometres long and fifteen kilometres across at its widest point. I also found out that the forest fire happened in 2011, the result of arson. Besides the extensive damage to trees, about a third of the town burned down. Almost four hundred houses and businesses, including an apartment complex, were destroyed. I probably heard about it on the nightly news back then, might even have followed the story for days, but unless I have some sort of relationship with an area, it is easy to replace it in my memory with more current stories. Rebuilding has happened and now it looks like a thriving town of ten thousand people.

As I leave Slave Lake, it's clear how the fire hit some areas along the highway and then jumped across the road, missing other sections. The new growth is everywhere and seems to be flourishing. In a few years, the new trees will hide the remaining blackened poles.

I'm driving west with the sun at my back. The sky is a lovely pale blue with many grey, fluffy clouds, the entire scene enhanced by the sun. The road gently rises then falls with the landscape. Sometimes it is slightly elevated, revealing hills in the distance on the far side of a modest valley. The sun illuminates everything in front of me and I'm aware of just how content I feel. This is a gorgeous drive. No traffic behind me, a pickup truck way out in front. I'm seeing scenery I've never seen before. When I drove on this road last night, I was headed in the opposite direction, a different perspective entirely.

Morning sky heading west from Slave Lake

Now, way off in the distance, the hills are blue. There are little farms with farm equipment and outbuildings. As I travel along, the colours change slightly, so now it's pale greenish-blue off in the distance and an azure blue above peeking through the clouds. There is texture everywhere. I pass the intersection of Hwy 33 where I came in last night and continue on Hwy 2 west heading for Kinuso and on to High Prairie. This is new terrain now.

Landscape heading west from Slave Lake

Everyone needs a chance to be by themselves now and then, to think thoughts they normally wouldn't think. For me, that opportunity for unfiltered thoughts has always been on the open highway. This morning I'm not thinking so much about the animals I hope to see but about the impact light has had on this trip so far. I'm remembering pictures I took on Hwy 5A between Merritt and Kamloops on Saturday, with the lighting doing wondrous things to the landscape, and again the following morning as I headed to Barriere and beyond. This morning everything is fresh and lovely, and I know it's because of the angle of the sun. It's important to have the light from the right direction when taking pictures, but this morning there is something else hovering just below my consciousness. It has to do with light. If I want to see the world at its best, if I want to notice more beauty, I need the sun at my back. Nothing new there, except I'd only thought of it in terms of photography before. Now I'm thinking if I want to see more beauty in general, I have to position myself in the right direction. Of course! But I'd never really thought about it before. And what if you could do that with life—what if there was some way to know which direction you should be going in life? If only! With writing, photography, or any creative endeavor, it's so easy to lose confidence in one's vision and give up. I want something shining on the path in front of me, telling me this is the direction. Is there any analogy to be found in this? Any way I can translate light and beauty into a life lesson? I keep turning it over in my mind as I drive along.

I just saw two deer. I saw two deer and I believe I got a picture. I'll see if it's clear enough to use.

About seventeen kilometres after Kinuso, I pass a side road with a sign indicating a police station. I can see the lake in the distance. I do a little U-turn and take that road. I would like to see more of the lake, and with a police station in the vicinity, this has to be a safe detour. I find a small community called Faust, park my car at the Faust Harbour Authority, and get out to walk around.

Harbour at Faust, Alberta

The air is filled with bird calls and the unique clanking sound of boats rubbing against their moorings. The water sparkles from the sunlight dancing on it. The woman who runs the Harbour Authority is on her deck smoking a cigarette. I stop in the sunshine and chat with her a bit, learning something about the area. Although I'm intentionally standing a good ten feet from her because I don't have a mask on, it feels almost normal, like in pre-Covid times, to be outside talking with another person. I bask in the familiarity of such an exchange. I have so missed normal interactions like this. I find out that Lesser Slave Lake freezes over in the winter. The ice gets about thirty inches thick. Imagine going skating on a lake this size.

Lesser Slave Lake and the harbour at Faust

There are four men out on a dock, or breakwater, with folding chairs and fishing poles. It is so peaceful, I long to join them. But instead, I get some snacks out of the trunk of my car, open a bottle of water, and start back on the road again.

Lesser Slave Lake at Faust

Heading west from Faust

    As I pull back onto the highway to resume my trip west, again I'm bedazzled by the canvas I'm seeing in front of me. The colours are so fresh and vibrant that the world feels filled with meaning.

    I just saw three deer running across the field to a clearing in the woods. I get what I believe will be a bad picture of them close to the woodlot far in the distance.

Three deer in the field near Faust, AB

As I get closer to High Prairie, the woods recede and the landscape is definitely more prairie-like. Little clusters of trees sit way back in the fields. Plowed ground. Beige stubble. Brown earth. A little bit of grass growing. There are still dandelions here and there, some gone to seed. Clouds, high sky, big sky. I love the openness of the land. In the winter, when it's cold and the wind is roaring across the open fields, it wouldn't be very pleasant, but in the spring, I really like it.

I stop at the A&W in High Prairie for tea and a break. I'm again aware of bird songs outside and think I should get a birdhouse for my property back in Surrey. Perhaps several. It's lovely to watch them and to hear their songs.

At 9:47 a.m., I turn onto Hwy 2 north. The road sign says McLellan is thirty-four kilometres away. I have never heard of this town.

The road passes through a wooded area for a while, and then back into wide open prairie. Fields have been planted, just a hint of crops starting to grow. High sky. So much space. The railway track is running beside the road. Intermittently, there is spacious farmland, and then heavily treed areas. Cattails grow beside the railway tracks. Red winged blackbirds use them as perches.

Alberta countryside

I'm aware that on this trip, I don't have the same curiosity about the rest of the world as I do for Canada. I have visited other countries and I've certainly enjoyed the experience, but it is Canada that has my heart. I think of countries in the same category as families. Other people should love their families/countries and I will love mine. Perhaps my curiosity comes from being born in Prince Edward Island and always being aware the rest of the country starts just on the other side of the Northumberland Strait. Whatever the reason, it makes my heart sing to be exploring parts of my country I have never seen before.

I turn north. The town of Peace River is only sixty-three kilometres away. Just as I make the turn, this field, planted and growing, looks emerald green with the sunlight on its leaves. I try to capture it with my camera. The colour is so rich and alive. To see something so memorably beautiful and to have no way to share it with others feels bittersweet. I can share a photo, yes, but it's not like sharing a book or a movie. The totality of this moment in this place cannot be passed along for others to enjoy. It's a banquet for those fortunate enough to be passing by now with time to stop and feast. Today, I dine alone.

Emerald green field on Hwy 2 north

I pass oil wells, their arms pumping. Within a kilometre, I see three clusters of these, reminders that I'm in Alberta.

Oil wells in Alberta

The sun keeps shining through the clouds and highlighting parts of the terrain. It reminds me of a play where the spotlight shines on one corner of the stage and then another. Or perhaps Disneyland. A Small World—and as your boat moves through the building, lights focus on various costumed dolls. Here a sunbeam breaks through the clouds and highlights a plowed field, rich brown earth, and next a grove of trees as the clouds move across the sky.

Why do I find plowed fields so beautiful? Am I alone in this? I love to see the contours of the land and how the light casts shadows over the furrows. And I also love to see swaths of stubble bent in opposite directions, showing the path of the harvester, a striped effect depending on how the light reflects from the surfaces. The colours, the subtle colours are wonderful.

As I get closer to Peace River, there is a big canyon or similar opening up ahead. The land of the prairies feels like something to be counted on—flat and solid. It's visually open with no hiding places. And now, it's unsettling to realize this land has so much depth that erosion can gouge out or sculpt something this deep across so many kilometres. Now the road is descending as if on a mountainside. Still moving down, steep hillsides curving down and around, and still going down. Like a big gap, an immense wound in the earth. Finally, there are buildings up ahead and a bridge.

Peace River is a town of almost seven thousand people. I drive through McDonalds for my tea, then move to the back of the parking lot for a thirty-minute nap. The townsite, I learn later, is nearly one thousand feet below the relatively flat terrain of the countryside surrounding it.

Peace River, AB to Dawson Creek, B.C.

I've been thinking about the difference between what I see and experience compared to what I can capture in photographs. Our personal reality is always going to be much greater than what we can communicate to others. For example, I have already seen more wildlife than I can share. I have few pictures, little proof. My best description cannot do justice to the reality of watching a deer bound off across a field. Therefore, whatever I show here will be at a lower intensity than my experience. It would follow, then, that as a society, our realities will always be richer and deeper than what we are able to convey to one another.

Some people might enhance their stories, but usually we notice the hyperbole and then we withdraw our trust. They are done! So, it seems that no matter how fully we try to share our response to the landscape, or anything in fact, it has to be less than the reality of the situation. We are each a hidden reservoir of rich experiences.

I do a U-turn to take a picture of an old barn or some type of silo. I stand by my car to stretch for a moment, and I see a deer by the driveway across the road.

Abandoned building near Fairview, AB

Deer emerging from a grove of trees

Time to turn on my air conditioning. Ah, lovely! It feels like such a relief to have cool air circulating.

Now I'm travelling south. Fairview is about thirty minutes away. I see a number of old abandoned buildings within a few kilometres. Another abandoned barn and house in a field. Stubble, perhaps from last year's wheat.

Abandoned house and barn

    This is a landscape of patchwork quilt. Very open. Beautiful big sky today. The clouds appear so close that reaching overhead to pluck one out of the sky seems a possibility. They are just floating there. Looking lovely.

Immense sky with clouds

I stop in Fairview at the A&W. The odometer reads 161,166. Funny how sometimes you can notice numbers line up in a way that seems relevant but isn't. I take a quick spin around the town and think it looks very nice for a community of three thousand. There is a curling rink, an arena, a good-sized library, and a downtown area that is at least three blocks long. I feel a bit reluctant sharing my purpose for being in Fairview. Anyone who has been watching Jordan Peterson's many videos over the past few years will recognize it as his hometown. I have a great deal of respect for him and thought it would be interesting to see where he grew up. Years ago, when visiting Manitoba, I made a point to see the home of Margaret Laurence, a writer I especially admired. As I was planning my route from Slave Lake to Dawson Creek, I realized that just above a straight line connecting the two points on the map was the town of Fairview. It would be an easy detour to include a brief stop here. If the only two people whose hometowns I'd seen were Margaret Laurence and Jordan Peterson, then in a way that does define me.

Fairview, Alberta

A street scene in Fairview, AB

Fine Arts Centre in Fairview, AB

I pass a college campus on the way out of town and then see a sign pointing to the Fairview Ski Hill. A ski hill on the prairies? I laugh aloud.

When I pull off to the side of the road to rid my windshield of dead insects (I just happen to have a bottle of window cleaner and paper towels in my trunk for this purpose), a deer walks out from the underbrush. I manage to get some pictures, but it would be easier to get one in focus if only the animal would pause for a moment. Unfortunately, it doesn't.

Highway scene heading south

I turn west on Hwy 49 heading to Spirit River. Just before Spirit River, I see another deer and get quite a few photos before it dashes off.

Deer bounding off across a field in Alberta

Alberta farmland

Many more kilometres and I'm checking into my hotel in Dawson Creek. It's lovely to pull back the covers and stretch out on the bed for an afternoon nap.

Later I meet up with a friend for dinner and he takes me out to see an old trestle bridge built in 1942-43 as part of the Alaska Highway. The historic Kiskatinaw curved bridge, a timber-truss structure about 122 metres in length, stands at Mile 21 of the Old Alaska Hwy.

Kiskatinaw curved wooden bridge

On the way back into the town of Dawson Creek, we are treated to a sunset almost as fine as the one I saw in Slave Lake.

Sunset over fields near Dawson Creek, B.C.

Today's Recap

Sightings: ....Deer – Five sightings

(group of two deer,
group of three deer near a woodlot,
three individual sightings)

Most memorable moment: ....Seeing an emerald green field

DAY FIVE –
Wednesday, June 9, 2021

Dawson Creek to Chetwynd, B.C.

IT'S NEARLY 10:30 A.M. WHEN I leave the hotel. My odometer reads 161,336. I'm quite familiar with Dawson Creek, having visited here a few times, although I'm really only acquainted with the main streets. The town has a population of around thirteen thousand, which makes it the largest place I've been to since passing through Kamloops last Saturday.

This morning I'm out of food. The cooler in my trunk is empty. Because of the Covid pandemic, I'm avoiding the inside of establishments as much as possible. So I drive through McDonalds for a tea and an Egg McMuffin. I'll be relying on drive-thru restaurants now until I get back home.

Everywhere I travelled after Hinton until I reached Dawson Creek—everything was fresh and new. Because this likely was the only time I'd be driving this route, I was as open as I could be to horizons, hillsides, rivers, and streams. I savoured every minute. But now it's suddenly lovely to have a sense of the familiar. I know where to find McDonalds, where to get gas, and where the turn-off is to go to Chetwynd.

I can only experience new things for so long before I am happy to welcome the soothing feel of the known. And as I think about familiar places, I see that I've missed my turn-off. I've accidently made my point about being less attentive when the surroundings are familiar. I circle back and take Hwy 97 west towards Chetwynd, my ultimate destination on this trip. It will be a short drive, only ninety-eight kilometres.

The countryside is spread out on either side of the road leaving Dawson Creek. More patchwork quilt fields, some green, some with old stubble, and others with the blush of freshly sprouted plantings. Trees along fence lines. I realize what I like about the farming countryside. The seasons are so distinct. Either the fields are ready to be planted, the crops are growing, it is harvest time, or a time of resting. When it's new, like now, it's so new. To see an entire field sprouting with new growth, the incredible abundance of seeds planted, and here it is stretched out in field after field. I feel a rush of tenderness towards the new growth as I would if seeing baby robins in a nest or newborn kittens groping for their mother's milk.

And the clouds—ever challenging in how to describe them. Clouds simply are not the same day after day. Today there is plenty of blue sky showing, but the clouds have arranged themselves in big tumbles. Like large plops of meringue on a lemon pie. Floating. Generously sized clouds. It's strange to think how much loveliness has been created as part of something that is a functional part of our weather systems.

Further along, I look out over hills and a great expanse of trees. I believe most of the trees are poplar. Here and there a field has been carved out of the treed expanse. Traffic is light.

About halfway to Chetwynd, there's an area to my left with mountains in the distance. Lots of open fields here with plenty of greenery and dandelions. Trees in full leaf along the borders of the fields, standing prettily in the sunshine. This is one of those places where I find the arrangement of mountains in the distance, the fields and fencing, clouds above with textures of light and shading, the entire lay of the land so picturesque that appreciation just wells up from my heart. It brings me great satisfaction to see it every time I pass through.

There is something about familiar landscapes that makes me smile. Rather like visiting an old friend, someone I've seen many times, and yet I'm still happy to see them again.

I've driven more than halfway to Chetwynd, and I've managed to do it without anyone behind me. The moment I see someone way off in my rearview mirror, I find a place to pull over and wait until they pass. So, no traffic behind me for the entire way, and nothing in front of me, which is my ideal way to travel.

From the landscape up ahead, there is a large rift in the land. This is similar to the deep division in the earth in Alberta near the town of Peace River. Here there is a brake check for large trucks, called East Pine North. The sign says the grade is six percent. The road winds downhill for three kilometres. I cross the bridge over the Pine River. Now for the long climb up the other side. I've driven this hill in winter with snow falling, silently praying, *Please, God, let me keep traction.*

A favourite scene on the way to Chetwynd

Highway heading to Chetwynd

    The clouds seem so extravagant at one point, I have to stop to take pictures. So difficult to pick a focus that avoids power lines but takes in enough of the scene to give a representation of what I'm seeing.

    There's another long hill to go down before I reach Chetwynd. My odometer says that Wabi Hill is also three kilometres long. I've come down this hill during a heavy snow and was very relieved when I reached my destination safely.

Now that I've arrived in Chetwynd, there is work to do. It's too early to check into my hotel so I make some phone calls to my tenants and property maintenance people from my car. I'm trying to find someone to cut lawns and do yard work this season.

Chetwynd to Hudson's Hope, B.C.

It turns out that most appointments work better for people tomorrow, so I'm left with time on my hands. I'm familiar with the road to Hudson's Hope, just sixty-five kilometres away, and I've seen wildlife on that route before. Ever hopeful, I set out on another drive.

Moberly Lake

I see a deer beside the road but there's no opportunity for a picture.

Then a big flash of lightning. It's not raining, but there is a large dark cloud overhead.

A moose! I see a moose in a grassy area beside the road, do a U-turn, and try some pictures through the window. He's just grazing and doesn't seem terribly disturbed by my presence. However, from experience, I know the sound of a window being opened, that change in tone, will often frighten an animal. When I am sure I have the best pictures I can get through the glass, I risk opening the window. I manage one photo before he turns and moves off into the forest.

Moose near Hudson's Hope (taken through car window)

I'm over the moon with happiness. It's rare to see a moose and wonderful to see one out in the open where I can actually get a picture. This seems to compensate for the many hours I've driven without seeing any wildlife on this trip.

It's single lane driving over the Peace River Bridge as road crews are cleaning off sand from the winter's road maintenance. Big bridge, immense canyon.

Hudson's Hope is a nice-looking community of around one thousand people. I'm just driving in at 3:05 p.m. when I get pulled over by the RCMP. *This is it,* I think, worried they noticed my license plate was from the lower mainland. Not only am I out of my health district, I'm not even in Chetwynd, my intended destination. I don my mask and roll down the window. Ah, speeding through a school zone. I had seen the posted speed sign and slowed to under 50 km/h, but I didn't see the second sign, the school zone sign, immediately after. I'm quite irritated with myself because I had noticed the high school, even watched students pour out from various doors.

The officer returns from his vehicle and hands me back my license, insurance, and a ticket. He smiles and says, "It's just a warning but it is on record. Have a good day." A warning—I'm so thankful it was nothing more. First a moose, and now this. My lucky day! Then I see another deer as I'm leaving town. From the size of her tummy, I'd say a new fawn should be arriving shortly. I get a few pictures.

Deer beside the road outside Hudson's Hope

On the way back to Chetwynd, I pass a bank of wild roses all in bloom. That starts me looking for others. I notice many but the others haven't blossomed yet. This will be lovely in a few days.

I check into my hotel with time for a nap before venturing out later.

Chetwynd towards Tumbler Ridge, B.C.

It's 7:45 in the evening. The sun, on its way to the western horizon, casts light from behind me. The trees are vibrant as I head out of town on Hwy 29 in a south easterly direction towards Tumbler Ridge. Time after time, parts of hillsides are flooded with light and trees cast long shadows across the road in front of me, while other trees shimmer in the golden rays.

What am I doing here?

What is it that I am really doing here? My intention had been to show people the pictures of wildlife and encourage them to do some exploring of their own. But on this trip so far, the scenery has taken top billing. In the past, I've counted many deer along this road. On one evening several years ago, I saw over twenty deer. Tonight, so far, nothing. Yet my heart is leaping over the sheer beauty of what's happening with the sunlight passing through the trees, intermittently blocked by clouds in the distance. It is engaging my senses in a way that is hard to describe and that I can't fully capture with my camera.

On the road to Tumbler Ridge from Chetwynd

On the road to Tumbler Ridge from Chetwynd

Whenever I've gone on a long trip by myself, it seems a theme will become apparent. As if the solitude of driving takes me to a meditative place not normally available. Sometimes I'm working through a problem and I'll get a glimpse of an answer while driving. It has happened so often that I've come to trust it. On this trip, I am intrigued with questions about light and I'm struggling to find a way to relate that to my life. So far, I can't make any connections between the two, but the desire hovers just below my consciousness.

Along the road to Tumbler Ridge

I've also been thinking about how every light-infused bit of scenery feels like I'm participating in an adventure. This has me reflecting on the nature of these experiences. Some of my greatest adventures seem quite ordinary. For example, feeling my newborn's grip on my little finger, or getting to know another person on a deeper level. When I walk away from a conversation feeling I've had moments of pure connection, that's when life feels rich with adventure. Then there are those rare moments, a numinous experience or an encounter with the holy.

Layers of history in the cliffs around the area

My intention was never to drive all the way to Tumbler Ridge so now I'm ready to turn around. The sun is in my eyes as I head back to Chetwynd. The light on the trees makes them look almost transparent, but I can't capture it because it's too bright. When I head directly into the sun, the landscape is still beautiful but somehow, I can't absorb the full impact of it. It's too much. Also, heading into the sun seems to blot out the wonder of the sky.

Today's Recap

Sightings: .... Deer – two individual sightings

Moose – one sighting

Most memorable moment: ....Seeing the moose

DAY SIX –
Thursday, June 10, 2021

Chetwynd to Mackenzie, B.C.

I HAD A FEW APPOINTMENTS in Chetwynd earlier this morning. I've had a good look around the building and made my "To Do" list. I'm a bit early for my one o'clock meeting, so I meander around the hillside for a few minutes. As I turn the car around in a cul-de-sac, a deer is lying under a tree just off to the side. Oh gosh! A noon nap. I take a few pictures of her. She notices me but doesn't move.

As I get out of the car for my next appointment, I see a deer on the neighbouring property. I take my cell phone to get pictures as the deer moves among several trees. Then she walks over onto my property and into the backyard. I quickly walk behind the building, taking the wooden stairs to the upper part of the lot. I can see her. She is grazing in an old dog pen enclosure, the gate of

Deer resting at noon in Chetwynd

which is wide open. She's only about twelve feet away and I wonder just when she will bolt. I stay still, my cell phone in front of my face, my finger pressing photo after photo. She stands quietly for a few moments, looking at me, then slowly takes one step, then another towards the opening from the fenced area. As she gingerly emerges, keeping her eye on me, I wait to see where she will go. Instead of bounding off, I am surprised when she takes another few steps towards me. And then she sinks down on her front knees. Is she okay? Is she hurt? I'm not sure what to do. She then folds her back legs and settles down under this tree just a few feet from me as if this is the most natural thing in the world. I am in awe.

Deer leaving old dog pen area.

Deer collapses onto her knees a few feet from me

Deer continues to collapse

Deer settles down under the shade of a tree in front of me

I take a few more pictures, then slowly turn and walk away as quietly as I can. A most amazing incident. When I finally meet with my tenant, I share this story. He says sometimes the deer come up to the building and press their noses against the window looking inside. A delightful story.

By two o'clock in the afternoon, my work is finished. I check my odometer at 161,712 and leave Chetwynd heading south on Hwy 97.

At first, there are a few farms on the way out of town. And then it's all trees and mountains.

Pine Pass is just over one hundred kilometres along the highway. Interesting fact—there are more than fifty mountain passes in British Columbia. I sometimes wonder if anyone has ever calculated the surface of B.C. because most of the province exists on the sides of mountains. I picture the province as a paper-mache project with the mountains split and laid flat. For a province with an immense area, there is a very small proportion suitable for farming or for communities. Unless someone has flown over B.C. or driven up north, it is hard to conceive of the great number of trees covering this province.

The air in my car feels cool as I near the pass. It's overcast. There is a slight drizzle, just enough to keep my windshield wipers on "intermittent."

Today is not a beautiful day, just as all days in life are not wonderful. I can recognize the beauty around me, but it is not stunning like some of the days on this trip. Today is more a day of potential. I can see the shape of the mountains and trees and I know when the sunshine comes along, this scenery has great promise. But the sunshine is not here right now. It simply remains as potential. Or a day of contrast. If all we had were beautiful days, then we would lose the awareness of that beauty, for there would not be anything to contrast it with. So I'm willing to settle for mundane days, overcast days, even welcome them, so I can feel the full impact of spectacular days.

This day might be mundane in one sense, but how do I categorize a day in which a deer has just settled down for a midday nap in front of me as if it was the most natural thing to do? I will remember that forever.

Further along the road, in a clearing down over an embankment, I see a black bear. I back up ever so carefully so I can get him in my camera sites, but he runs off. So close! Disappointing! I should note that I have no idea whether the bear is male or female. For some reason I wrote "him" without much thought. I think I prefer guessing incorrectly rather than saying "it."

Then soon, I see another bear. This one is on the move, and I have a clear picture for a moment, but I hit the wrong button on my cell phone. The place where I'm pulled off is a recreational area of some sort. There is a building out here in the middle of nowhere. Perhaps a lodge or camping facilities. I don't really pay attention. I'm grappling with my camera now, turning it on. There are people over near the building. I hear shouting, "There's a bear."

Then a woman's high-pitched voice. "Where? Where is the bear? I don't see it. Where is the bear?"

In my head, I am silently screaming at her to shut up or she'll scare the bear. And, of course, the bear moves quickly across the open area to some bushes near the water. I manage to click one picture before the bear disappears into the underbrush. If only they had been quiet, I could have taken some good pictures. Still, despite her ruining a perfect moment, the whole episode feels like high adventure. I inhale deeply, knowing there is a self-satisfied smile on my face.

Bear heading into bushes

Now I'm coming to the turn-off for Powder King Ski Hill. It's raining heavily, but I don't care. I'm happy about the bear sighting.

I pull off the road at Biloxi Falls. I get out of the car in the rain to the roar of the water crashing down the mountainside. It's quite overwhelming to see the torrents of water rushing down over the rocks and disappearing under the roadway.

Biloxi Falls

When I reach the turnoff for Mackenzie, I decide to turn right onto Hwy 39 and go into the townsite. It is twenty-nine kilometres away, and it seems to be a good time to pick up some food. Also, I have been along this road once before and saw two black bears. Will I be fortunate again today? It is raining lightly with a dark cloud up ahead.

New growth along the road into Mackenzie

No bears this afternoon. When I came through here before, there had been a lot of beetle kill and the trees were being cut down. Now new growth has filled in and the area is looking quite good. Mackenzie is an attractive little town of almost four thousand people. The townsite was established in 1966 by two forest companies. On my previous visit, I spent time driving around the town. Today I stop in front of the Subway, put on my mask, and go inside to order my sandwich. It's interesting that I don't feel lonely travelling about the countryside by myself, but carefully standing six feet away from servers in masks makes me feel lonely to my core. Behind these masks, we are less than strangers. We are also anonymous, lacking identity.

Mackenzie to Prince George, B.C.

I head back out to Hwy 97 and on towards Prince George. Soon I come to Tudyah Lake on my right-hand side. It is quite a large lake and in the past, I have taken photographs of it. But now the trees by the side of the road have grown tall and are so thick that I can only see the lake through the trees. Which brings me to a favourite rant of mine. Why can't departments of highways recognize that roads do more than connect people?

Highway south to Prince George

Yes, I know that highways connect towns and villages and make transportation of goods and services possible. But does no one realize that beauty feeds the soul? These glimpses into the sheer beauty of our landscape can have an impact on our happiness and well-being. When a highway rounds a corner and opens up to a whole valley floor spread out below, it should be mandatory that a safe viewpoint be established. And when the highway lingers beside a lake like this one, there should be pull-outs and bushes cleared from the shoreline so we can enjoy that beauty. And if the department in charge of running telephone lines could kindly put the telephone poles on the other side of the road, where they won't ruin the view, I would be most appreciative. To create spaces for people to experience the awe connected with visually stunning landscape should be at least as important as getting them safely from one location to another.

I decide to drive into McLeod Lake to get gas. I turn right and cross over Pack River on a little one lane bridge. McLeod Lake is First Nations land, and the gas station is only a couple of kilometres from the highway. I have been here before. But my timing is not good, and it is closed for the day. That's fine as I have more than enough gas to get to Prince George.

I hit a big downpour and quickly pass through it.

Scenery between Mackenzie and Prince George

Scenery between Mackenzie and Prince George

After miles of nothing, it seems a surprise when I see buildings and a sawmill. It turns out to be Bear Lake, a small community with a population of less than two hundred people. Then I'm into wilderness again. Just before I come to the Salmon River, I see two animals run across the roadway out in front of me. Full grown coyotes or young wolves? I can't tell from this distance.

Farm country north of Prince George

This section of Hwy 97, from Prince George all the way to Dawson Creek, is also known as the John Hart Highway. The highway is named after the former British Columbia Premier, John Hart. Eventually, I come into farming country and there are more signs of population along with highway. I have hotel reservations in Prince George for the night but no idea where I will sleep tomorrow night.

I check into the hotel, text my family that I've arrived, and get busy transcribing what I've recorded during the day.

DIANA M. MOHRSEN

Today's Recap

Animals viewed: .... Deer – two individual sightings

Black bears – two individual sightings

Coyotes or young wolves – two

Most memorable moment: .... The deer lying down in front of me

DAY SEVEN – Friday, June 11, 2021

Prince George to McBride, B.C.

IT'S 8:43 ON FRIDAY MORNING. My odometer reads 162,085, and I have a full tank of gas. It's a bright day, an almost clear sky. This morning at the hotel, I was told that one Covid restriction has been lifted and the dining room is now open. Breakfast is included in the price of the room, so I head to the dining room. Technically it is open, but it doesn't feel that way. I am the only person here. Anything I choose has to be taken with me. I decide on a bottle of juice, a banana, a croissant (in cellophane), along with two small packages of cheese in heavy plastic. One small step on the way back to normalcy, I suppose.

I leave Prince George over a long bridge spanning the Fraser River. I'm headed for McBride, 204 kilometres to the east. No communities in between, except possibly a farm or two, nothing more. A lot of blue sky.

I see a coyote. It looks quite young. It starts to run across the road but there is oncoming traffic. It turns and runs back. After the vehicle passes, it bolts across in front of me. As I brake, my car starts the ding, ding, ding to indicate that I'm low on washer fluid. There are no gas stations nearby.

Deciduous trees beside the road. Little bushes, shrubs. Evergreens behind that. Tall spires reaching up to a sky filled with clouds. I've left the clear skies of Prince George far behind. Some of these clouds are dark, menacing, while others are white, illuminated. Perhaps I'll stay in Valemount tonight. I'm thinking of driving over to Jasper again as I'd love to see mountain goats or big horned sheep. I could do that, then return to Valemount. No matter what I finally decide, I will be back home tomorrow night.

Logging trucks come towards me, heading to the mills in Prince George. This road is usually very quiet, but not today. Another double long logging truck, and another. Another. All within three or four minutes.

Between Prince George and McBride

The road curves down a hillside, snow peaked mountains off in the distance, and another mountain range in the other direction. The mountains are far enough away to appear a darkish blue, medium blue sky above. The sun is shining once again. No driveways. Just wilderness. I like the bushes beside the road. The sun is glinting off them and making them look transparent, silver, sparkling and shimmering. Another logging truck is heading towards me. I cannot see any signs of a logged area but obviously there is a lot going on.

As I drive along, the mountain peaks change. Now they are tall with craggy peaks topped with snow.

A big black bear is on the road ahead. I pull over and stop. It runs across the road in front of me then disappears down the bank on the other side. And then, in what seems like a miracle, it turns and comes back onto the road. I manage to get several pictures before it disappears again.

Black bear on roadside between Prince George and McBride

Before I start the car, I reach out for my cell phone. It's not on the seat. I dig down between the seats. Not there either. I look on the dashboard, in my purse, between the seats again. Now I'm forced to consider moving the passenger seat to see if it slid underneath. That means getting out of the car, walking around, and opening the side door—the side where the bear just disappeared. I can't see where it went. What if it's just out of sight over the embankment? I don't want to walk around the car and discover it is still there. What to do?

I do the only thing that seems reasonable. I take everything from my purse, put it on the seat, and then return it to my purse. No cellphone. It must be in this damned car. Finally, I get out, leaving my door open. I quickly open the other door, push the seat forward, feel underneath, move it back, and repeat. No phone. Now I'm getting angry. I can't possibly have lost a cell phone in the excitement of seeing a bear. There, on the floor, face down, black cover on black floor mats, up under the dashboard, is my phone. It must have slid off the seat when I saw the bear and hit the brakes. Twenty minutes of wasted time.

Back on the highway, a deer skitters across the road in front of me and down over the bank. It looks quite young. Whenever I brake, it throws the washer fluid level off and I have to listen to the ding, ding, ding again. Yes, I know, add washer fluid.

I keep hitting little pockets of rain, and then it clears. I suppose it makes sense. If I drive over two hundred kilometres, I will encounter different weather along the way.

As I enter McBride, a deer is standing by the road nibbling away on leaves.

McBride is a village of just over six hundred people. It is in the middle of this broad, flat valley with mountains on either side. The woman in the tourist bureau tells me this valley runs between the Canadian Rockies to the north and the Cascade Mountains to the south. Why have most people never been through the Robson Valley? I've talked to those who have never heard of this area. I order tea and a slice of banana bread at the café next to the tourist bureau.

Farmland near McBride

McBride, B.C. to Jasper, AB

I've been travelling east, facing the sun, this whole morning, and I'm finding it hard to accept I'm not going to get any good pictures. The scenery is great, but the lighting is off and I can't do anything about it. I see a large field with buttercups everywhere and long to take a picture. I restrain myself because if the light isn't there, I won't be satisfied with the results. I'm still trying to connect this with life, but if there is a connection, it eludes me. Sometimes things happen easily or are more satisfying as if they were meant to be. Is there any way of knowing beforehand? Some sort of signal?

When I reach the intersection with Hwy 5, instead of turning south towards Valemount, I make a quick decision to continue east to Jasper. By now, the sun will be at my back instead of directly overhead like it was earlier. I think if I drive all the way through to Hinton, AB, and stay overnight, then tomorrow morning I can come back this way with the sun lighting my path. I realize this is a little insane, as I just drove this same route last Monday in the pouring rain. It will make it a very long day to go from Hinton to Surrey tomorrow, but it can be done. It will be worth it if I see some wildlife.

I'm sitting on a little side road with a great view of Mount Robson. There are clouds in the sky, and I'm waiting for the sun to reappear. If it does, I expect it to shine on the snow at the top, making it a great picture. I read my book for about ten minutes, but it doesn't happen the way I'd hoped. Instead, the clouds slide over around the top of the mountain. The restaurant at Mount Robson is closed. I'd planned on getting my food there as they usually have great choices. I hadn't considered it might be closed because of Covid. I get a couple of bottles of water in the gift shop connected to the gas pumps. I also pick up washer fluid and fill the reservoir. I've been listening to the ding, ding, ding reminder of low washer fluid for too many kilometers now. I will welcome the quietness.

At Moose Lake, I take some pictures of the lake and the mountain. I wish I knew the names of the different mountain peaks.

In Jasper, I need to find some food. I can see that there are people in restaurants, so I choose one, put on my mask, and go inside. I sanitize my hands at the entrance and follow the waitress to my table. The tables are spaced out nicely for the Covid restrictions.

After leaving Jasper, I pull off to the side of the road to photograph a mountain. I've just eaten Moussaka, probably the worst Moussaka I've ever eaten, along with a Greek salad with partly browned lettuce. The meal came with a bowl of lentil soup, which I took to go (I don't even like lentil soup), and a tea. $26.70 so I left $30, a sad little tip, but not worth half that amount. I have such mixed feelings. It was wonderful to eat in a restaurant again after such a long prohibition, and yet such a disappointing meal. A cellophane wrapped sandwich from a gas station would have been preferable.

It feels like dusk as there is very heavy cloud cover, but the sun hasn't yet set. Far from it. I can see the top of the mountains.

Mountain in Jasper National Park with a train passing by

There are places in the park where big horned sheep frequent. I go to the first place, pull to the side of the road, and turn off my car. My thought is to read my book and wait, hoping some animals come down off the mountain to drink. I read and wait. Read and wait. Nothing.

Jasper National Park

Okay, I'll carry on to the next place of possibility. As I drive along, something catches my eye to the right, across a lake. I pull over. Four adult mountain sheep and a little one are at the water's edge. Really too far away for my little camera but I do my best. They are there. I've seen them, and that counts.

Mountain goats in Jasper National Park

I wish they were closer. I exhaust my photographing possibilities and reluctantly decide to leave.

In Jasper National Park

I spend some time taking pictures of the various mountains in the area.

In Jasper National Park

Scenery in Jasper National Park

When I come to a place where several cars have pulled off to the side, I pull over too and then I see them. On the rocky cliff front, high up, two male big horned sheep and three young ones. I don't see any females around. I don't have to rush with my pictures as the animals seem to be content where they are.

Big horn sheep in Jasper National Park

A second big horn sheep in Jasper National Park

One sheep gets up and moves

Three young big horn sheep

This was what I came to Jasper National Park for. There is no point in going on to Hinton. Instead, I'll return to Valemount if I can phone and secure a room for the night. So, I turn around, and soon see a mountain goat on a mountainside by itself.

Mountain goat in Jasper National Park

Mountain goat in Jasper National Park

Jasper, AB to Valemount, B.C.

I have no cell phone coverage until I reach the town of Jasper. I call ahead and book accommodations in Valemount for the night. Just after passing the Jasper townsite, I see an elk by the side of the road. And another one just outside Jasper.

Elk grazing in Jasper National Park

In a clearing down over an embankment, I spot a very young fawn. A quick picture as it runs off into the trees. I'm doubtful anything is in focus. No adults in sight.

At 8:30 p.m., I'm passing Moose Lake heading back to Valemount. It's getting dark because of that heavy cloud cover even though the sun will not set for another hour.

A herd of elk to my left. I quickly pull over and grab my camera. They disperse just as quickly, but I'm guessing there were eight to ten of them. I manage to get pictures of the back end of several of them.

Herd of elk

I haven't had the radio on since I left home seven days ago. And I haven't turned on the TV in my hotel room, not even once. The only sounds in the car have been me singing fragments of songs (badly). That, and the sound of the tires on the road. It is very restful not hearing the daily news or Covid statistics.

Today's Recap

Sightings: ....Coyote

Black Bear

Deer – two individual sightings

Mountain Goats – four adults and one juvenile in a group,
and one individual sighting

Big Horn Sheep – two adults, three young

Elk – two individual sightings,
one herd of eight to ten,
Fawn

Most memorable moment: ....Seeing both mountain goats

and big horn sheep

DAY EIGHT –
Saturday, June 12, 2021

Valemount to Merritt, B.C.

IT'S PARTLY SUNNY AS I leave Valemount. The odometer is at 162,693. I slept in this morning. It's a little after nine o'clock when I swing through the Tim Hortons' drive-thru for my tea and a breakfast sandwich.

This morning when I got into the car, I had the strange thought that I might be caught "avoiding traffic" in the way that I do. Not that I'm doing anything wrong, and I'm careful to pull over safely. But it was the feeling of being discovered, of having my true motives uncovered. I imagine a voiceover by some distant authority. "There's a woman who keeps pulling off the road to let the traffic go by. Ah, we get what she's doing. She's not really driving at all. She's just looking at the scenery and animals. We'll have to put a stop to that." Alone with my thoughts, sometimes nonsense shows up. There have been other times, while on a long drive, when moments of profound insight break through, times when I go back home renewed, more often than not.

There is a special mountain on the road south of Valemount. Several years ago, I took what is one of my favourite pictures. Since then, I've been trying to find the name of the mountain peak, so far unsuccessfully. Part of the problem is that I'm vague about exactly where along the highway I saw it. Conditions on that day were perfect for photographing this particular mountain, and today I'm hoping I will see it so I can note the precise location. But this morning, the mountain peaks are partly obscured by cloud, which makes it difficult to pick out the same mountain. To add to my difficulties, it was completely snow-covered in my photograph, and today there is a bit of snow on more than a few mountains.

Mountain peaks with cloud cover south of Valemount

    Moisture is evaporating from the ground. I can see wisps of mist or fog slowly rising. I can't get a good look at any of the mountains to identify their outlines. I spend most of the drive from Valemount to Blue River—a distance of ninety kilometres—playing "Could this be the mountain? Or perhaps this one?"

    By the time I reach Blue River, it is raining lightly and the clouds are still playing havoc with my goal of identification. I only know for sure that I took that picture before I reached Blue River. Obviously, I'm not going to identify the mountain on this trip.

I've talked quite a bit about letting traffic go by in order to have the road to myself. I should also mention that there are times, like now, when there's a long mountain road with curves and double lines but no obvious place to pull off. Under these conditions, when I see a vehicle come into view far off behind me, I pick up the pace. I drive like a normal human being who wants to get somewhere as quickly as possible. I can do that quite competently and ignore any regrets over what I might be missing.

I pass a sign telling me it is thirty-nine kilometres to Avola and 229 kilometres to Kamloops. Kamloops is about five hours from home if I don't stop to take pictures.

The bridge at Avola spans the North Thompson River. The water looks quite calm today. And here are the same lupins (pinks, blues, and purples) I noticed on the way up to Valemount on Sunday. They remind me of PEI where banks along the highway are covered with various colours of lupins. The sun is shining on them, inviting me to take a picture. So I do.

Lupins

Just south of Avola, I notice a large pond where I saw the two swans on Sunday. I stop again, hoping to get a better picture. Today there is not just one pair of swans but two pairs. The water is so still, it's like a mirror. Unfortunately, it's also reflecting back all the lovely light, and it is too bright to get a picture.

I've been noticing construction intermittently along the route from Valemount. Are they widening the road or building a pipeline? The swath of trees at the side of the road has been removed. Units of heavy equipment have been working at a number of locations. I'm stopped by a flag person as a truck moves across the road. I roll down my window and ask. He tells me this is all work for the pipeline. I'm glad something has been happening while so many businesses have been shut down due to Covid.

Highway scene heading south

Around the community of Vavenby, the area opens up into a bit of a valley. The road is elevated and off to my left, a few little farms are carved into the forest. The sun is shining and has brightened everything. A hawk hovers over the highway. The road continues down and around the mountain. There have been quite a few cut blocks logged on the opposite mountainside. Trees are at various stages of regrowth and reflect the light differently, so it gives some contrast in colour. Add to that shadows from clouds overhead, and it has a dappled effect overall.

I decide to stop in Clearwater, in the actual townsite, not at one of the fast-food places along the highway. This is a small community with fewer than 2,500 people. Today there is a farmers' market in progress and plenty of vehicles around. I don't know where I'm going and take a turn hoping to get closer to the beautiful lake that gives the town its name. I see a sign for the Painted Turtle restaurant and follow the road to see if it is open. And it is. What a find! It's right on the water. Irises are growing along the lake front, which is sprinkled with lily pads. All dappled in sparkling sunshine. It looks like a Monet painting. I choose a table by the lake, take out my book, and read until my meal arrives. A single Egg Benedict with homemade hash browns. The whole experience is delightful.

Clearwater in front of the Painted Turtle restaurant

I leave the restaurant feeling very appreciative and head out onto the highway. Before long, I see four little ducklings on the pavement heading to my lane. I take a deep breath, fearing the worst, but they do an about-turn and reach the ditch before being squished by oncoming traffic.

Eventually, I pass a sign that says, "Thank you. Come again." I'm puzzled. Where have I been that I should return? It's been just road and trees for some time now.

At the rest stop in Little Fort, I clean out my car. Sandwich wrappers, plastic water bottles, a brochure for Wells Grey Park, scrunched paper towels with the remains of dead bugs from my windshield. All of this has been accumulating on the floor of the back seat. The air outside is warm and filled with fluff from the cottonwood trees. I take a picture of the trees.

Cottonwood trees near Little Fort

I love the land around Little Fort. The road is elevated on one side of the valley. The flat farmland is down below next to the river. The fields often get flooded by the North Thompson. If there is standing water on the land, there can be lovely reflections. The shoulder of the highway along here is really not adequate to pull off far enough. I do take a bit of a risk sometimes if no one is coming behind me. I'll pull off and quickly take a photo through the window, then continue on my way. I like the big, rough terrain of the mountains on the far side of the river, rocky outcrops with a few fir trees sprinkled here and there. Then the soft, new growth of the flatlands down by the river. Again, I'm frustrated that our highways don't leave opportunities so we can fully enjoy the landscape. It is like taking an escalator through an art gallery. No stopping, keep moving. Watch your step. Ridiculous!

Just as I'm complaining aloud, I see a side road angle off to the left. I try it. It is a little country road that leads to a couple of farms. There is a cattle guard across the road, and a little marmot has poked its head up between the bars. We are at a standoff. I'm sitting in my car, idling, and the marmot is sitting on the bars of the cattle guard. Neither of us move. I take a few pictures, wondering what he/she will do next. It disappears back underneath, and I drive on.

Finally, I'm down on the flat farmland, able to take the pictures I want. There are wild roses along the roadway and clover in the fields. My windows are now fully open, and the scent is amazing. I'm not sure if it's from the roses or the clover, possibly a mixture of both. I must remember this road in case I'm ever back this way.

Air filled with the scent of wild roses and clover

There's something about stepping foot onto the land that fixes a location in my mind more firmly than merely turning down the window and taking a picture. Here I have the luxury of being on a country road with no traffic, so I am able to get out of the car and take a few minutes to absorb it. There's a game I play sometimes, just to shake up my view of life. I remind myself of exactly where I am. For example, right now I'm in a place I've never been. I've never walked on this road before. The day is not too hot, and it's not too cold. The sun is just shining down sweetly, and I can feel it warming my face and arms. The air is fresh and filled with a scent I inhale deeply, trying to identify it. My heart feels light, and I'm filled with contentment. And while I am here, in this particular spot, I'm also on a planet that is spinning at 1,670 km/h and moving through space on a great arc around the sun at over 100,000 km/h. If I concentrate on the reality of this for a minute or two, I will be able to recall later on how it felt to stand here beside a field in the interior of B.C. on a spring day in 2021.

Countryside

Back on the road, I eventually see a sign that says Barriere Forest District. Just up ahead near the river is that abandoned farm I love, the one I took pictures of a few days ago. If ever I win the lottery, I will buy this property just for the sheer love of the location. But since I never buy lottery tickets . . .

Cottonwood trees are abundant, especially along the riverbank, with fluff blowing everywhere. When I pass through Barriere, the cottonwood fluff is particularly noticeable. Like snowflakes drifting through the air.

Hills around the Kamloops area

I've noticed on this trip that every small community has managed to get its cannabis outlet in operation despite Covid. Yes, everywhere, it seems.

I breeze through Kamloops, don't stop at all. I guess I'm in "home" mode now. I continue on Hwy 5 south to Merritt. I do love the landscape in this area. I wouldn't want to live here as it's too cold in the winter and too hot in the summer, but I do adore these hillsides. I would love to be able to paint them, to capture the colours.

Merritt to Surrey, B.C.

It's 2:52 p.m. when I get to Merritt. The odometer is 163,100 as I fill up the car for the rest of the ride home. I'm feeling just a bit road weary, so I take the McDonalds' drive thru and order a bottle of water and another tea. Then I park the car under an elm for shade and slide the seat back. I'm not wanting a nap here, just a change of pace. I stretch out my legs and open the bottle of water. Cold. So refreshing. I brought two books with me on my trip and have been concentrating on just one. This time I reach for the other book, one I've not opened for weeks, and continue from the page marked with a green Post-It Note. I read the following sentence: "The sense of meaning is an indicator that you are on that path." I look around my car as if seeking confirmation from someone about what I've just read. Is this a universal joke? I was looking for some indication about the rightness of a particular path. That the next page in a book I'd not found time to read for weeks, if not months, would have the precise answer I was looking for seems to be too much of a coincidence. The book is *Beyond Order, 12 More Rules for Life.* The author, Jordan Peterson, is referring to a path of maximum virtue. While maximum virtue wasn't part of my question, I wonder if a sense of meaning could provide the confirmation I was looking for, like sunlight highlighting the beauty of our surroundings? I'm very familiar with what a sense of meaning feels like. I had just never put it together with any decision I was trying to make. But to use it as my guide? Could I do that? My tiredness lifts, and I can feel excitement bubbling up. This at least could give me a way to navigate some of life's questions. If I go in the direction that feels meaningful, I can later decide if that really has been helpful.

I leave Merritt for the final stretch of my journey. Now that I've had a bit of a break, it once again feels like a relaxing ride. I move the steering wheel a bit and touch my foot to the gas pedal, but that's about it. I'm not darting in and out of traffic. I'm not waiting for passing lanes. I'm just floating along in my magic-carpet car, enjoying the scenery and thinking how glad I am to be living in this particular time in history when a woman can just get in a car and safely travel over a great swath of countryside. A hundred years ago this couldn't have happened. And a hundred years in the future? I'm doubtful. I suspect people will be forced to travel by public transport unless they're extremely wealthy.

I enjoy the wilderness of the Coquihalla, so many square kilometres of unpopulated mountainous land. As I go down Larsen Hill, I remember seeing a black bear along the river years ago. As I near the bottom of the hill and the river, the tree growth is now so thick, I would not be able to see a bear even if there was one there.

There is still snow on the mountain peaks as I pass the summit. Just after the snow shed tunnel, I pull over and take several pictures. The shades of green on the mountainside in the sunlight are lovely.

South of the snow shed on the Coquihalla Hwy

As I drive, I'm still thinking about how particular things seem meaningful. It's not like I decide to make them meaningful. Rather, it's as if they already exist as having meaning for me. Waiting for me to discover them. I think back to Hwy 5A and to all those pictures I took. I wanted to share the beauty of that area because the beauty itself felt filled with meaning. And I think about this book. Instead of asking myself what if it's a waste of time, I now change the question to whether it will be meaningful to me to create this book. Yes, it would.

I stop two more times, once in Hope for a bite to eat and again in Chilliwack to have a quick visit with a friend.

It's 7 p.m. when I pull into my driveway. It's been a long day, and I'm more than ready to relax in front of the TV for the evening. My odometer shows 163,360. I've travelled 4,360 kilometres in eight days. My wanderlust has been satisfied for some time to come.

I curl up in my favourite chair and turn on a recorded program from my TV. I can't shake the memory of picking up that book and reading, "The sense of meaning is an indicator that you are on that path." I wonder now if I had read it earlier, weeks and weeks ago, and it's been gestating in my mind. I will never know for sure. I only know that after searching for days for some analogy to illuminate my travels, this sentence has had an impact above and beyond what it would have had if I had simply read it as part of a page, part of a chapter.

There's a quote I once came across by philosopher Martin Buber. He said, "All journeys have secret destinations of which the traveler is unaware." I've often come home from a trip with a new awareness or the answer to some problem. It is both mysterious and wonderful how travel can provide us with experiences beyond our expectations. I hope it is so for others as well.

Today's Recap

Sightings: .... Swans (two pair)

Four ducklings

Marmot

Most memorable: .... Lake at Clearwater (Monet painting)

The End

CPSIA information can be obtained
at www.ICGtesting.com
Printed in the USA
LVHW071722200922
728849LV00009B/207